DUTCH ENTERPRISE AND THE VOC 1602·1

# Dutch Enterprise and the VOC

1602·1799

HARM STEVENS

WALBURG PERS

With thanks to Annebet van Duinen (*Tobacco and the VOC*), Martine Gosselink (*Other end of the world*), Daniel Prins (*Story of an East Indiaman*), Alfred Staarman (*Mars and Mercury: one ship, two masters*) and Hans Wildeboer (*New hosepipe fire extinguisher*).

*Cover: View on Batavia* by Hendrick Jacobsz Dubbels, detail from *View on Batavia Castle* by Andries Beeckman, *Grenadier's mitre of a VOC-soldier*, eighteenth century.

*Translation:* Sammy Herman
*Design:* Frederike Bouten, Utrecht

CIP/ISBN 90 5730 019 2

# Contents

**DUTCH ENTERPRISE AND THE VOC 1602·1799**


6 *Introduction*
DUTCH ENTERPRISE AND THE VOC 1602-1799

9 *Dirk Hartogs was here*
AN ACCIDENTAL ARRIVAL IN AUSTRALIA

15 *Mars and Mercury: one ship, two masters*
THE ARMED MERCHANTMEN OF THE VOC

21 *Story of an East Indiaman*
THE FLEET, THE ENGINE OF THE COMPANY

27 *Sign of authority*
HIERARCHY, DIFFERENTIATION AND DISCIPLINE ON BOARD

31 *Tragic loss of the Hollandia*
SHIPWRECKS: THE VOC'S FAILURES

37 *New hosepipe fire extinguisher*
HIGH TECH FOR THE VOC

43 *Significance of a pin*
DIVISION OF LABOUR IN THE EIGHTEENTH CENTURY

47 *Silver for export*
THE VOC AND THE GLOBAL MONEY MARKET

53 *Importing porcelain*
THE VOC AND EUROPEAN TASTE

59 *Importing textiles*
CHANGING FASHIONS AND THE VOC

65 *Tobacco and the VOC*
COMMODITY, GIFT, WAGE OR RATION?

71 *Commerce and arms*
THE MILITARY APPARATUS OF THE VOC

77 *Profits and piety*
THE VOC AND RELIGION

81 *God's word in Arabic*
THE VOC AND THE ASIATIC LANGUAGES

87 *Other end of the world*
THE VOC'S OVERSEAS BASES

91 *Women and the company*
DUTCH EX-PATS IN ASIA

# Introduction

Perhaps the most famous words ever written by the nineteenth-century writer Conrad Busken Huet are at the close of his book *Het Land van Rembrand*: 'Java and the *Syndics* are actually the two best credentials we have'. While the Netherlands has Rembrandt to thank for the *Syndics*, the nation's connection with the island Java is mainly due to the Dutch East India Company (Verenigde Oostindische Compagnie or VOC), which traded between Asia and the Dutch Republic for two hundred years from its foundation in 1602. And the Rijksmuseum continues to profit: Huet's credentials are preserved and displayed in the museum. Rembrandt's *Syndics*, or the *Sampling Officials of the Drapers Guild* and other highlights of Dutch art are on view in the painting department. Objects and paintings connected with the VOC are exhibited in the Rijksmuseum's Dutch History department.

The Rijksmuseum's collection includes a variety of items that were formerly part of the Company's own collection and that of the stadholders. Because of their origins, these exhibits reflect an official image of the VOC. In particular, they relate to the political-institutional and military aspects of overseas history. If this were all that the Rijksmuseum's VOC collection had to offer, it would present a fairly one-sided view of the Company; these paintings and objects reveal little about the everyday order of business within the VOC, about the material aspects of trade or about the technology that the VOC had at its disposal.

To fill the gaps a programme of expansion was initiated in the 1970s to broaden the collection with finds from the wrecks of VOC ships. The Rijksmuseum was the first Dutch institution to express an active interest in marine archaeology, a relatively new scientific discipline whose achievements represent an important source of information about the material culture of the VOC. Placed in the context of the Company, these material remains provide an insight into the way business was done in practice. As a result of this expansion the Rijksmuseum's present VOC collection offers a more rounded and comprehensive reflection of the enormous diversity of activities of the Dutch East India Company.

For this volume an arbitrary selection has been made from the collection. Material remains of the age of the Dutch East India Company form the basis of the chapters in which various aspects of how the VOC functioned are discussed. Yet however arbitrary the choice, one thing is clear: the VOC was a complex organisation with many different facets. It was both merchant and shipowner, as well as shipbuilder; in some parts of Asia it was regarded as a kind of sovereign; at sea, but also on land, the VOC was powerful and feared; moreover, as a transport company the VOC was the principal intermediary between Europe and Asia, bringing goods and people – and with people, ideas – from one continent to another. The VOC was a multinational *avant la lettre* with trading posts spread throughout Asia and Africa; a modern company that set high standards in products and equipment, and was therefore in touch with the cutting edge of technology.

Clearly, therefore, the historical phenomenon of the Dutch East India Company is far from simple. In fact the world of the VOC forms something of a mosaic, with the objects, paintings and drawings shown here in their historical context representing authentic remains of that mosaic. The material heritage bequeathed by the Company has enabled subsequent generations to assess the different facets of the VOC's history in their true perspective, free of the colonial, and indeed anti-colonial rhetoric, and free of today's fashionable search for the sensational which has led to early overseas history being portrayed as a caricature, a simplistic story in which shipwrecks, scurvy, keelhauling and gin are the order of the day. Behind the stereotypical image of empire-builder, exploiter or primitive, but tough old sea dog lies a different story of a more sophisticated VOC.

It is the tangible heritage of the VOC and the knowledge accumulated over the centuries about the subject that reveals a modern company, by the standards of its own day, involved in a tremendous diversity of activities. A company, moreover, that played a major role in European expansion, one of the most significant processes in world history of the last five hundred years. The history of the Dutch East India Company, as the exponent of Dutch culture, is therefore of international importance. That is why Huet considered Java – the centre of the Company's operations in Asia – to be one of the nation's two best credentials. . . . . . . . . . .

1616
VAN AMSTERDAM
DE 27 DITO
NA BANTVM

# Dirk Hartogs was here

## AN ACCIDENTAL ARRIVAL IN AUSTRALIA



In August 1611 the East Indiamen *Rode Leeuw* and *Gouda* arrived in the roadstead at Bantam. The voyage from the Texel roadstead had taken – excluding a brief pause at the Cape of Good Hope – five months and 24 days. That was a record. Commander Hendrik Brouwer had taken his ships by a new route.

Until then the Dutch East India Company had always followed a course that led from the Cape of Good Hope, via the island of Madagascar to Mauritius. From there it was straight sailing, practically parallel to the equator, across the Indian Ocean to the Sunda Strait, the passage between Sumatra and Java. This final leg could take considerable time. Winds could suddenly drop around the equator and cause long delays. Heat and thirst exacted a heavy toll among the crew, too.

Brouwer decided on a different tack. At the Cape he sailed south until he came to a latitude of between 35° and 40°. Here constant westerly winds blew the whole year round, and swept Brouwer's ships east. When he thought he was at the right longitude for the Sunda Strait Brouwer changed course and sailed north. Once in Bantam, Brouwer compiled a report on his new route for the Heren XVII. Following a series of successful voyages using the southern course, the directors passed a resolution on 4 August 1616 ordering all VOC ships in future to sail the route Brouwer had discovered six years before.

Sailing this southern route was not without its dangers. Ships were not equipped with navigational instruments that could determine longitude. Calculations were based on estimates of distances and directions travelled. And this was how the master decided when the moment had arrived to change course north, for the Sunda Strait. Dead reckoning, as this form of calculation was known, could often result in an estimate that was quite different from the actual position. A master who waited too long before steering his vessel north risked brushing the western coastline of Australia, although no one knew this in those first years following Brouwer's voyage: apart from the northern shores, for Europeans, Australia was *terra incognita*, the treacherous west coast had yet to be discovered by Europeans, let alone charted. The advent of the southern route and the inaccuracy of longitudinal calculations meant that a confrontation with this landmass was just a question of time.

In 1616 the inevitable happened. Skipper Dirk Hartogs sailed his ship, the *Eendracht*, so far east on Brouwer's route that in October of that year he sighted

◀ Pewter plate with inscription: *1616 on 25 October there arrived here the ship the Eendracht from Amsterdam, senior merchant Gillis Miebais of Liège, Skipper Dirck Hatichs of Amsterdam having set sail on the 17th ditto for Bantam, the trader Jan Stins, helmsman Pieter Dookens van Bil anno 1616*
This plate is the oldest object of European origin to have been found on Australian soil.

land. Hartogs decided to turn this chance occurrence to advantage. He anchored off one of the islands along the mainland and subjected the place to a thorough two-day examination. Before lifting anchor and continuing his journey to Bantam, he placed a sign proclaiming his short visit to the island. Hartogs had found little of value on the island, and what he left behind was equally valueless: nailed to a pole was a pewter plate, beaten flat and inscribed with a text. A common, everyday utensil marking an event of major historical importance: the discovery of the west coast of Australia. Since then, the island has been known as Dirk Hartog Island.

There were many masters who, like Hartogs, sailed too far east from the Cape and found themselves off the Australian coast. In the course of time parts of the western coastline were charted – sometimes at a terrible cost, since the treacherous reefs made the area a potential ships graveyard. In fact it was soon apparent that an accurate chart of the west coast was urgently required. Indeed, this was an assignment which could be paired with an examination of the commercial potential of this unknown terrain.

It was the ambitious VOC governor general, Anthonie van Diemen (1636-1645), who commissioned the structural exploration of the Southland, as this *terra incognita* had become known. Abel Jansz Tasman was to take command of the expedition with the specific aim of 'sailing around the partly unknown and uncharted South and Eastland [...] to the greater improvement and aggrandisement of the Company's general welfare'. On 15 June 1643 Tasman returned to Batavia after a voyage of ten months. The results were not what Van Diemen had hoped for: expectations had been raised too high. Certainly, it had now been proven that the Southland – henceforth known as Hollandia Nova or New Holland – was not attached to the Antarctic continent and could be circumnavigated, as Tasman had shown; yet the discoverer had brought little news about the land itself, about its inhabitants and its commercial potential.

With Van Diemen's death the search for new markets and unknown countries came to an end. For the present, at least, because in 1696 and a new attempt was made to explore the southern continent. The expedition was led by Skipper Willem de Vlamingh, while Nicolaas Witsen – scholar, burgomaster and director of the VOC's Amsterdam chamber – was a formidable backer. The immediate motive for the attempt was the disappearance of an East Indiaman, the *Ridderschap van Holland*.

During the expedition led by Willem de Vlamingh in 1697, Victor Victorsz made small paintings of the South-land, as Australia was known. The top (No. 12) shows Dirk Hartogs' anchorage, and the place where Hartogs and his men first went ashore in 1616. On the right is the site of the pole with the plate that Hartogs left behind. The inscription reads: 'this is where the pewter plate was found'. Watercolour by Victor Victorsz, 1697. Maritime Museum 'Prins Hendrik', Rotterdam.

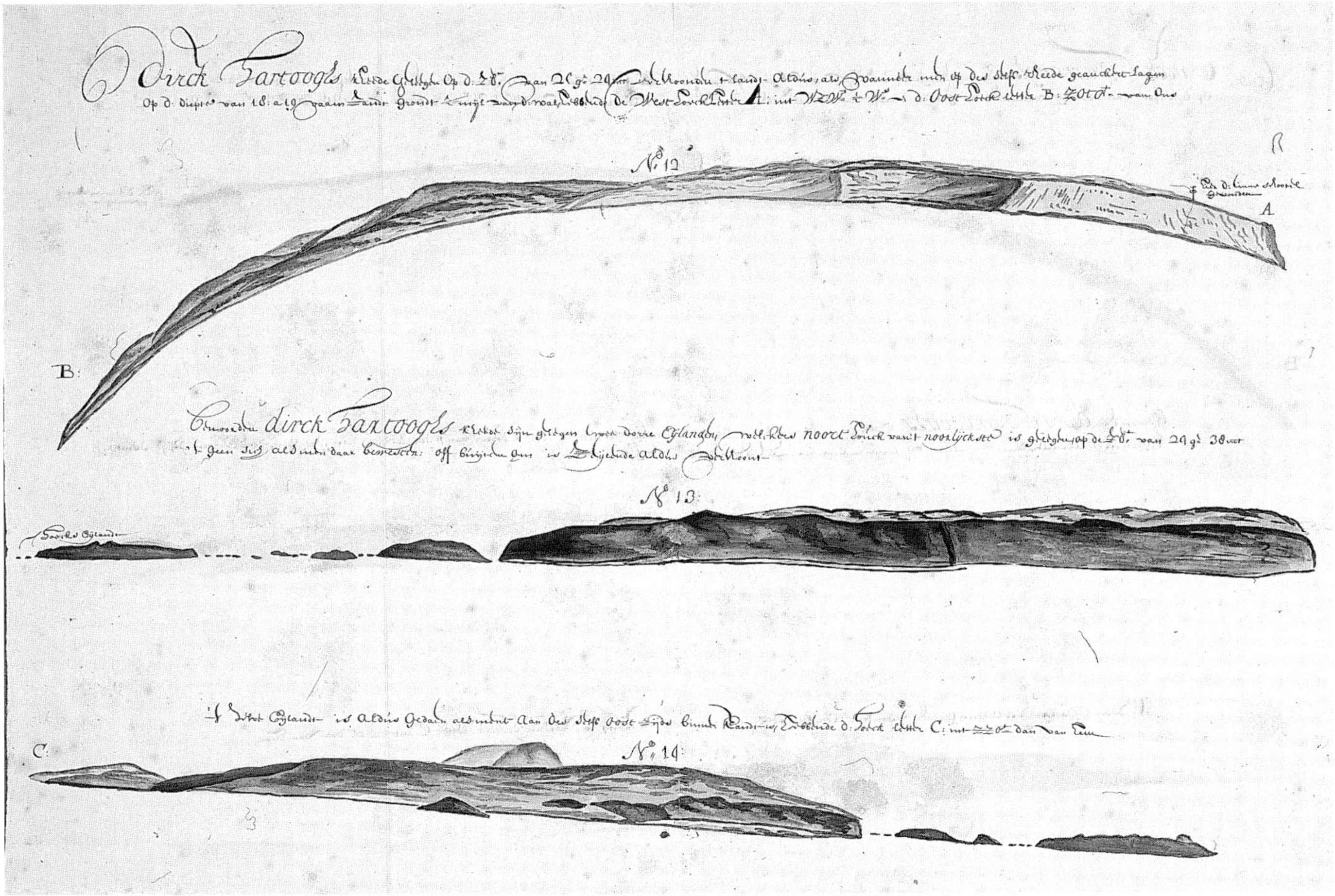

Antonio van Diemen (1593-1645), Governor General (1636-1645). Van Diemen encouraged efforts to explore Australia. In 1642 an expedition led by Abel Tasman left on Van Dieman's initiative. Anonymous painting, second half seventeenth century.

The search for this ship offered a magnificent opportunity to chart the western coast of Australia. Nautically the voyage was certainly a success. De Vlamingh's precise observations gave Isaac de Graaf, the Company cartographer in Amsterdam, sufficient information to draw a detailed map of the west coast of Australia. But apart from this information, De Vlamingh's exploration of the area led to equally few tangible results.

Nevertheless, De Vlamingh did not return empty-handed. During his visit to Dirk Hartog Island a remarkable discovery was made. As helmsman Michiel Bloem climbed one of the hills, he stumbled on a pole. Beneath the pole, half covered by sand, was a pewter plate. The inscription left no room for doubt: this was the same flattened dish that Dirk Hartogs had left behind eighty years before to mark his visit to the island. De Vlamingh and his men honoured Hartogs' gesture by placing their own dish on a pole exactly where the original had stood, with an inscription commemorating the two Dutch visits of 1616 and 1697.

Hartogs' dish was taken to Batavia, where Governor General Willem van Outshoorn decided to send it back to the Republic. This was duly undertaken on 30 November 1697; and so the first object of European origin to have been found on Australian soil was brought back to its native country, having left as a household utensil, it returned as a historical relic. . . .

# Mars and Mercury: one ship, two masters

What it was that enabled European countries to obtain a position of overwhelming power in Asia from the sixteenth century is not an easy question to answer. One thing is certain: a decisive part of the process was played by the European cannon. Thanks to the technological developments of the fifteenth century, Europeans commanded a level of firepower that was unmatched in Asia. Non-European nations consistently failed to close the technological gap in the field of arms production. This allowed the relatively sparse crews of the heavily-armed European ships to dominate the coastal regions of vast areas of Asia.

It was mainly the European countries along the Atlantic seaboard that managed to take advantage of this head start – especially Portugal. This maritime nation was the first to found a colonial empire in the

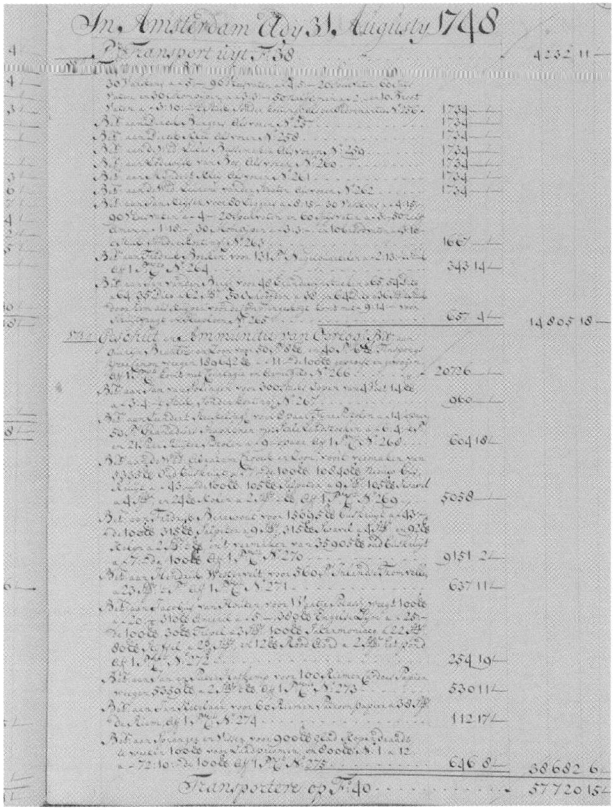
In Amsterdam Adij 31. Augustij 1748

Transport uyt F. 38 ... 4232 11

Geschut en Ammunitie van Oorlog ... 20726

Transportere op F. 40 ... 57720 15

Divers recover a 24-pound calibre cannon from the wreck of the Witte Leeuw. The East Indiaman sank in 1613 in Kerckbaai (Jamestown Bay) off St Helena in an armed engagement with Portuguese ships.

Journal of the senior bookkeeper of the Amsterdam Chamber of the voc, 31 August 1748: *Guns and ammunition for war. Paid to Quirijn Brants. en zoon for 50 ps. 8lb and 40 ps. 6lb. Finspongs iron Cannon weighing 189642 lb, at 11.- per 100 lb tested and weighed 1 pcto. deducted for Courtagie and Poor Relief No 266 20726*

Merchants Quirijn Brants en Zoon delivered fifty iron cannons made at Finspong in Sweden with a total weight of over ninety tons to the voc. The supplier was required to have the quality of the cast iron assayed before the sale at the municipal assaying yard. In addition, the exact weight of the guns had to be determined at the weigh house. One per cent of the price went to the poor relief fund. Algemeen Rijksarchief, The Hague.

sixteenth century and for many years the Portuguese dominated intercontinental trade. The first Dutch merchant ships to arrive in Asia discovered the Portuguese to be formidable competitors. The founders of the Dutch East India Company were more than conscious that any attempt to increase Dutch trade in Asia would inevitably lead to armed conflict with the Portuguese. This realisation resulted in the right granted by the States General to wage war in areas in which the Company held a monopoly of trade. In this way, trade with Asia was turned into a weapon against the Spanish and Portuguese – it was the continuation of the continental struggle of the young Republic against Spanish domination in a maritime context. Grand Pensionary Johan van Oldenbarnevelt claimed that there were two main reasons for forming the Company: 'To damage the enemy and to secure the homeland'.

Certainly in the initial years of the VOC's existence no real master plan existed aimed at combatting the Portuguese. Instead, a series of incidental armed confrontations occurred which eventually came to represent a kind of organised piracy on the part of the VOC: the object being to capture the cargos of enemy ships. In 1611, for example, the East Indiaman, the *Witte Leeuw*, took part in an expedition to the Philippines; in the course of the voyage five Spanish ships were taken. Two years later – now homeward bound – the *Witte Leeuw* became embroiled in a skirmish with two Portuguese ships lying at anchor in Kerckbaai (Jamestown Bay) off St Helena. With brash confidence the VOC ships (two vessels accompanied the *Witte Leeuw*) took up positions opposite the Portuguese ships. According to the Portuguese records, 'they made loud signs of joy with their trumpets when it became apparent that their prize could not allude them. Then both sides began the fight with volleys of gunfire'. But in their greed the Dutch became careless. In an awkward manoeuvre to try and board the Portuguese ships, one of the guns on the *Witte Leeuw* exploded. The fire spread to the powder room and the entire rear section of the ship was blown into the sky: the vessel sank with all hands lost.

The officers on board the *Witte Leeuw* had overplayed their hand. And it had cost the Company a precious cargo of pepper (perhaps as much as 100 tons) and Chinese pottery. Four years later the memory was still fresh. In the general instructions issued by the Heren XVII in 1617 to their merchants, the following words of warning were given: '... without risking ships too carelessly or allowing any other un-

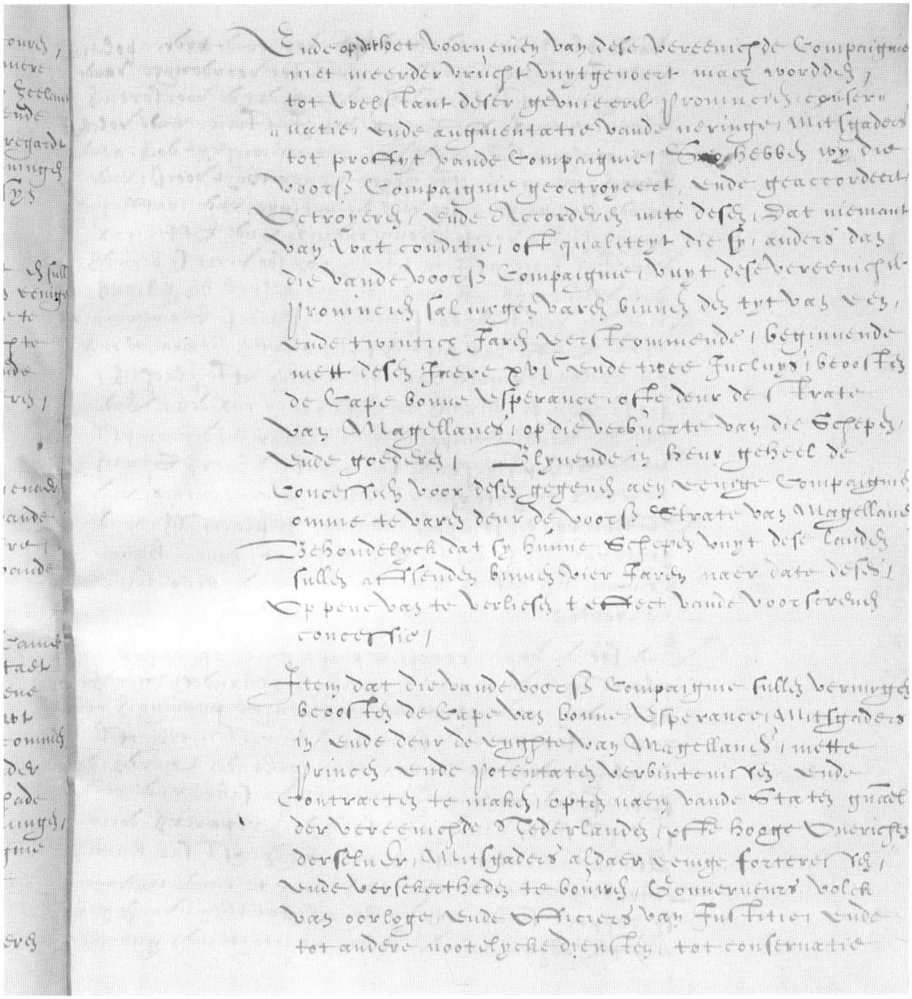

Extract from the charter of 20 March 1602: *Item. That those of the aforesaid company shall be authorised east of Cape las bonne Esperance [Cape of Good Hope] as well as in and through the Strait of Magellan to make agreements and contracts in the name of the States General of the United Provinces with princes and potentates, or with government officials, as well as to build fortresses and strongholds there and to appoint Governors, military personnel and Justices and other necessary services for the Conservation of the place, the maintenance of proper order, administration and Justice principally for the encouragement of trade.*

According to its charter the Dutch East India Company was allocated a monopoly of trade in the area east of the Cape of Good Hope to the Strait of Magellan. The charter also outlined the authority with which the States General had invested the VOC. The Company could conclude treaties with foreign rulers. The Company could also build fortresses, appoint governors and maintain an army. All, effectively, to maintain order in the interests of trade. Algemeen Rijksarchief, The Hague.

foreseen damage, just as, God spare us, in the encounter of the *Witte Leeuw* and two other ships with the two Carracks off the island of St Helena ...'.

The story of the *Witte Leeuw* had shown that aggressive tactics could seriously damage the commercial interests of the VOC. It was a dilemma that had plagued the directors of the Company from the start – and one that had direct consequences: the East Indiaman was both a merchantman and a battleship; and therefore both a commercial and a military target. The development of a satisfactory compromise between an efficient carrier of cargo and a powerful platform for a row of guns

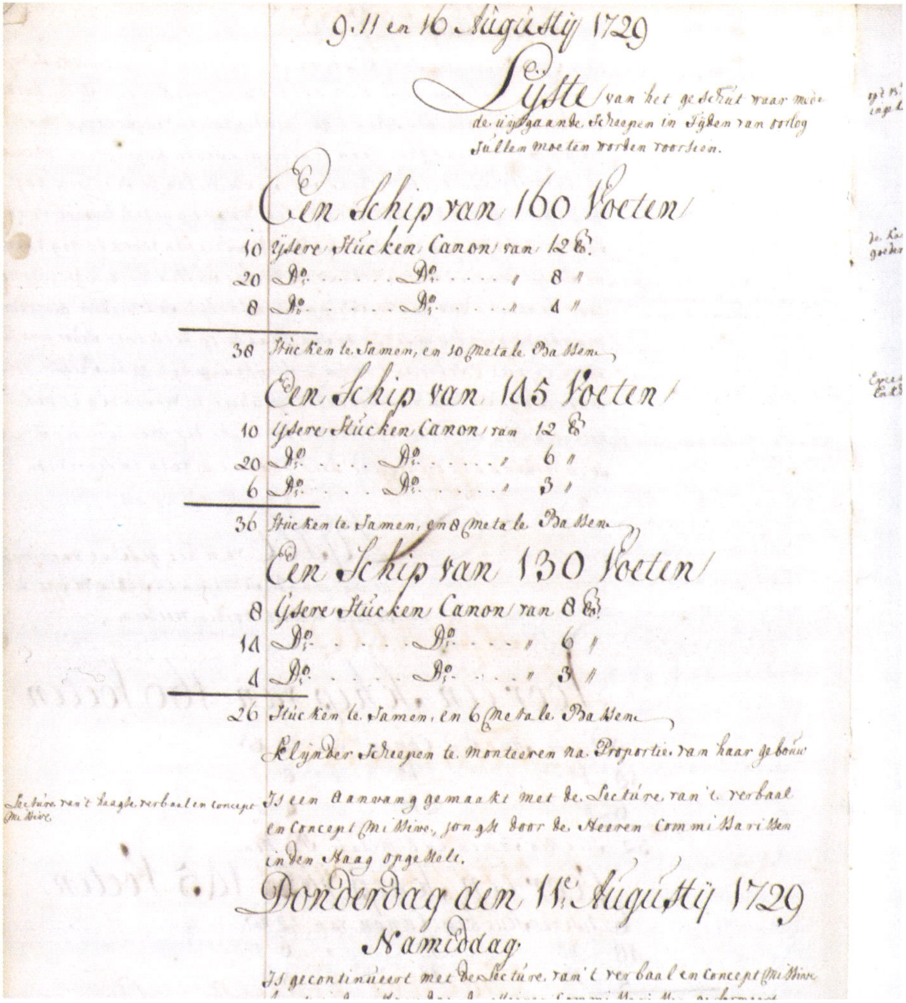

9. 11 en 16 Augustij 1729

Lyste van het geschut waar mede de uytgaande Schepen in Tijden van oorlog sullen moeten worden voorsien.

Een Schip van 160 Voeten

10 IJsere Stucken Canon van 12 lb
20 Do ... Do ... 8
8 Do ... Do ... 4

38 Stucken te samen, en 10 metale Bassen

Een Schip van 145 Voeten

10 IJsere Stucken Canon van 12 lb
20 Do ... Do ... 6
6 Do ... Do ... 3

36 Stucken te samen, en 8 metale Bassen

Een Schip van 130 Voeten

8 IJsere Stucken Canon van 8 lb
14 Do ... Do ... 6
4 Do ... Do ... 3

26 Stucken te samen, en 6 metale Bassen

Kleynder Schepen te monteeren na proportie van haar gebouw

Is een aanvang gemaakt met de lecture van 't verbaal en concept missive, jongst door de Heeren Commissarissen in den Haag opgestelt.

Donderdag den 11e Augustij 1729

Namiddag

Resolutions of the Heren xvii, 9 August 1729:

*9, 11 and 16 August*
*List of the guns with which ships shall be equipped when departing in wartime.*
*A ship of 160 feet*
*10 iron cannons of 12 lb*
*20 Do ... Do ... 8 lb*
*8 Do ... Do ... 4 lb*
*38 guns in all, and 10 metal swivel guns*

*A ship of 145 feet*
*10 iron cannons of 12 lb*
*20 Do ... Do ... 6 lb*
*6 Do ... Do ... 3 lb*
*36 guns in all, and*
*8 metal swivel guns*

*A ship of 130 feet*
*8 iron cannons of 8 lb*
*14 Do ... Do ... 6 lb*
*4 Do ... Do ... 3 lb*
*26 guns in all, and*
*6 metal swivel guns*
*Smaller ships to be equipped in proportion to build.*

The Heren xvii established which guns should be allocated to particular voc ships. This summary reveals that a ship of 160 feet would be equipped in wartime with 38 cannon and ten swivel guns (small guns for combat at close quarters). Algemeen Rijksarchief, The Hague.

remained a constant and urgent problem for the Company. Resolutions issued by the Heren XVII determined the number, calibre and type of cannon to be carried on the VOC's ships. This eventually led to an extensive standardisation of the artillery of the VOC fleet.

In time of war, or threat of war, ships carried extra guns. There was a continual awareness of the political and military situation in which the Company operated. In the 1680s the costly policy of maritime expansion, in which the fleet had played a vital role fighting, blockading and landing troops, came to an end. Now that the Company had established a hegemony in the Asiatic seas, there was no longer any need to send ships to the East equipped for war. In future, the military task of the VOC's vessels would be on a smaller scale: combatting pirates and Asian opponents who did not have heavy, modern European guns. In the late seventeenth century cuts began to be made in the artillery on Company ships; in fact, heavy guns had always had the disadvantage of reducing the amount of goods an East Indiaman could carry. Originally, ships were installed with guns to fire a maximum of 24-pound cannonballs, in the eighteenth century this was reduced to twelve pounds. The total weight of guns and munitions on board an East Indiaman diminished from 100 tons in the mid-seventeenth century to around sixty tons in the mid-eighteenth century.

The armed merchantmen was the instrument with which the VOC acquired its trading empire and held it. When, in the late eighteenth century, other European powers acquired the means to send modern warships to Asia to protect their commercial interests the end of the VOC's domination in Asian waters was at hand. Mars and Mercury, two masters on the same ship – it had gone well for two hundred years, but in the end the alliance was to fail.

Liefde (Love), *Vrede* (Peace), *Vrije Zee* (Free Seas), *Tortelduif* (Turtledove), *Jonge Prins te Paard* (Young Prince on Horseback), *Goede Fortuin* (Good Fortune), *Rode Leeuw* (Red Lion), *Zwarte Leeuw* (Black Lion), *Groene Leeuw* (Green Lion), *Rode Leeuw met Pijlen* (Red Lion with Arrows), *Boterbloem* (Buttercup), *Wassende Maan* (Waxing Moon), *Rad van Avontuur* (Wheel of Fortune), *Lands Welvaren* (National Prosperity), *Vriendschap* (Friendship), *Dankbaarheid* (Gratitude), *Standvastigheid* (Determination), *Voorzichtigheid* (Prudence), *Kijkuit* (Observance), *Aap* (Monkey), *Recht door Zee* (Straight and True), *Buiten Verwachting* (Exceeding Expectations), *Vlijt en Zoetigheid* (Work and Pleasure) – all names of East Indiamen. The Heren XVII revealed something of their artistic side here: it was they – not the various chambers – who decided in closed meetings on names for the new Company ships. Geographical names of the various cities and provinces in which the chambers were based were a regular choice. *Amsterdam*, *Middelburg*, *Hollandia*, *Hoorn*, *Walcheren* – in mid-ocean the men on these ships could still enjoy the illusion, however far they sailed, of being home.

Another example of this kind of reference to origins is revealed in a seventeenth-century ship model. At the bottom of the counter is a portrayal of a Zeeland town: a permanent reminder of the country the ship left behind when it sailed to the far-off Indies.

This townscape is not the only unusual detail on the stern of this ship model. A carved wooden figure was also part of the decoration. This represented Prince William II. It was after this Stadholder that the Zeeland chamber had named the ship which was built in Middelburg in 1649 under the direction of shipwright Cornelis Speldernieuw. On 5 May 1651 the *Prins Willem* left Rammekens roadstead at Middelburg for its maiden voyage to the Indies. Although William II had come to an untimely end, his wooden image on the stern of the ship still had a few stormy years to go. The spectacular career of the East Indiaman *Prins Willem* would see to that.

By the time the *Prins Willem* returned to Zeeland waters on 18 June 1652, the First Anglo-Dutch War had started. Because the Republic's fleet needed warships, the States General and the Heren XVII agreed that fifty East Indiamen would be temporarily seconded to the battle fleet. The *Prins Willem* was one of these ships. In the seventeenth century there was nothing unusual about the state employing VOC ships for naval purposes. Ships were exchanged both ways. During the Twelve Year Truce

◀ Seventeenth-century model of the East Indiaman Prins Willem. The original ship was commissioned by the Zeeland chamber of the VOC at Middelburg in 1649. During the Battle of the Downs in October 1652 the Prins Willem formed part of the Republic's fleet. As a merchantman the Prins Willem made fifteen voyages between Europe and Asia. On 11 February 1662 the ship sank off the island of Brandon in the Indian Ocean on its return to Europe.

The stern of a copy of the model of the Prins Willem. The painted town profile is clearly visible. Model by Herman Ketting.

(1609-1621) for example, the States General ordered the admiralties to transfer seven of their first rate men-o'-war to the Company.

To make it fit to serve as a warship the *Prins Willem* required considerable adjustments. The artillery which, for a large merchantman like the *Prins Willem* stood at around 32 guns of various calibres, was increased to around forty. To accommodate these extra guns a number of new gunports had to be cut. This was done at the front of the orlop deck where there was space for six ports.

The *Prins Willem* was ready for action and in October 1652 underwent a baptism of fire with the Republic's fleet at the Battle of the Downs. Indeed, for a while the *Prins Willem* even served as the flagship of Admiral Witte de With. Somewhat the worse for wear, the vessel returned to port where it was restored to its original function as a merchantman. The powerful forty-gun artillery remained, however. This was the end of the short military adventure of the *Prins Willem*.

As a VOC merchantman the vessel completed another fifteen voyages from Europe to Asia and back, as well as calling at various Company bases in Asia. On 23 December 1661 the *Prins Willem* left Batavia roadstead as part of the homeward-bound fleet under command of Arnold de Vlaming van Oudshoorn, member of the East Indies Council. It was to be the ship's last voyage. On the night of 10 to 11 February in the year 1662 the *Prins Willem* sank together with three of the fleet's other ships off the island of Brandon in the Indian Ocean. According to François Valentijn's account, the bad news woke Governor General Joan Maetsuyker from his sleep; he had been tormented by a vision in his dream. 'On the 11th February 1662,' wrote Valentijn in his volume *Oud en Nieuw Oost-Indiën*, which appeared in the 1720s, 'this gentleman dreamt that he had seen the honourable Arnold de Vlaming van Oudshoorn, member of the East Indies Council and commander of the fleet that had left Batavia on the 23rd December 1661 for the Republic, in terrible danger, and had heard the honourable gentleman call out several times for help. His excellency was so disturbed by the dream that he had woken up as a result.'

The *Prins Willem* had been afloat for around twelve years. Compared to the average lifespan

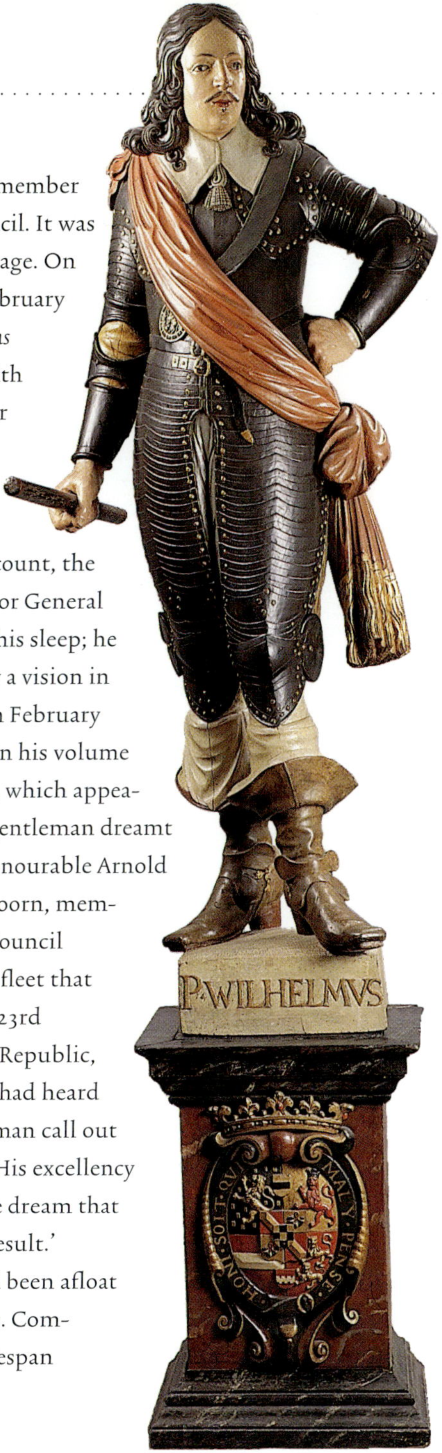


Prince William II, Stadholder from 1626 to 1650. This figure may have served as an example for the carving on the stern of the Prins Willem. Attributed to François Dieussart, c. 1650.

Model of the voc shipyard at Oostenburg in Amsterdam. Measured by the standards of its day, the shipyard was the largest in the world.

of ships sent out by the voc – some fifteen or twenty years – this was not especially short. The maintenance, renovation and improvement of its fleet of ships was a constant problem for the voc. Throughout the entire period of its existence the Company sailed more than 1,772 ships. Large East Indiamen like the *Prins Willem* formed the core of the fleet, but there were many smaller types of ship, including pinnaces, galliots, flutes and the various harbour vessels that the Company included on its register.

These ships were the engine that kept the Company moving. They were essential for the transport of goods and personnel, as well as for communications between the nerve centre in the Republic and the Asian bases. Decisions regarding the building of ships were taken at the highest level, at meetings of the Heren XVII. The directors were constantly attempting to achieve uniformity and standardisation in the fleet – it was important to know how much cargo a ship could carry – and to make the equipage and supply of ships as efficient as possible.

Most of the VOC's ships – as many as 1,581 – were built at shipyards run by the chambers of the Company. The Amsterdam shipyard on the manmade peninsula of Oostenburg was the VOC's principal local supply depot and its most impressive complex. In the late seventeenth and early eighteenth centuries, it was a unique example of far-reaching investment, with much of the funding going towards mechanical tools needed for the production of ships such as industrial windmills, lathes, advanced cable installations. The major increase in size, the concentration of fixed and liquid capital, the extensive division of labour and the high level of organisation at Oostenburg complete the image of an unusually modern enterprise. Measured by the standards of its day, Oostenburg's production capacity was the largest in the world.

## Sign of authority

'The Policy of the Company hinges on the prognostications of Mr van Dam on the IJ ...'; the words of the late-seventeenth-century poet Sylvius. From 1652 to his death in 1706, Mr Pieter van Dam was the VOC's legal advisor. Throughout these years he attended all the meetings of the Heren VII as secretary. Thanks to his long association with the Company and his expert knowledge of its workings – both at home and overseas – Van Dam managed to attain the influential position to which Sylvius referred. On 9 July 1693 he was commissioned in a resolution of the Heren XVII to 'compile a pertinent and accurate description of the constitution, administration and business of the Company, from the very start'. Van Dam spent eight years on this assignment, finally producing a series of eight volumes, each containing around five hundred pages: an encyclopaedia of a hundred years of the VOC. Van Dam's *Beschyving* contains a mass of factual information which is often presented to the reader without any apparent structure. In one of his casual asides he mentions an instrument known as a *sifflet* or boatswain's call: 'For many years it was customary to give *sifflets* to skippers, officers, quartermasters etc. down to the rigger, gilded and silver respectively, although when it was discovered that they were not being used, the practice was eventually abandoned.'

A boatswain's call is a pipe or whistle. A silver example was among the objects recovered from the wreck of the *Witte Leeuw*. That the boatswain's call had already lost its functional role at an early stage of the VOC's history (the *Witte Leeuw* sank in 1613) is obvious from this example. It must have been almost impossible to produce a sound of any volume with this whistle. One of the loops with which the chain is attached to the whistle is fitted loosely into a drilled hole, so that the whistle leaks. Moreover, there is no connection between the piston (the section with which the pitch was adjusted) and

Silver boatswain's call, or sifflet, Netherlands (?), c. 1600, found in the wreck of the Witte Leeuw (sank in 1613). From its shape it appears that it would have been impossible to produce a sound with this whistle. The object was mainly carried as a symbol of authority.

Quarterdeck on an East Indiaman. An awning is spread over the deck to provide shade from the bright, tropical sun. Behind the wheel is the entrance to the officers and passengers' cabins. Drawing by Jan Brandes, second half eighteenth century

the bowl, which probably originally included a pellet, where the sound resonated. As a result, the piston is useless.

This boatswain's call was therefore unusable and was worn on a long cord around the neck as an honorary symbol. It was especially popular in the latter half of the sixteenth and early half of the seventeenth century. Later, the *sifflet* gradually regained its original function as boatswain's whistle. On VOC ships the chief boatswain – the *hoogbootsman* – held the rank of petty officer. It was his task to supervise the entire crew. He did this in coordination with the rigger – the *schieman*. The boatswain was responsible for the running and standing rigging, particularly at the main mast, while the rigger's task was literally to keep an eye on the foremast sails.

Boatswain and rigger, like the others on board ship, formed part of the rigid hierarchical structure on the standard East Indiaman. In theory, it was the senior merchant who held supreme power on board. But because trading no longer took place on the ship, the senior merchant's official position in relation to the skipper did not reflect the situation in practice. When this fact eventually received official recognition in 1742, the merchant lost his supreme authority to the master. The latter was now also incorporated onto the ship's council where the projected course and disciplinary matters were dealt with. The boatswain also sat on the council since, as a petty officer, he was directly in touch with the crew; he was expected to know exactly what was going on.

Responsibility for navigation, and carrying out the skipper's orders lay with the ship's petty officers or mates. The helmsman also supervised the stowage of goods and the maintenance of the ship. Another of the petty officers was the junior merchant. His job was mainly administrative: keeping the ship's accounts and the muster roll, a register of the names of the entire crew. Distribution of food and drink – a weekly ration for everyone on board – was in the hands of the steward, who also supplied victuals to the cook. Maintenance of the ship, the sails and the barrels in which food was kept was the task of three craftsmen who had the rank of mate: the carpenters, sailmakers and coopers. The Heren XVII appreciated the importance of reliable technical personnel. From 1650 the position of craftsmen at sea gradually improved; indeed, moving tools without authorisation was a flogging offence.

In charge of order and dispensation of punishments was the marshal. He kept any member of the crew suspected of a crime prisoner, acted as prosecutor and was charged with carrying out punishments. Guidelines for disciplining offenders were contained in Articles issued by the States General, an extensive list of ordinances which applied to staff of the VOC for as long as they remained in the Company's employ. Before the ship departed, the men were required to swear to obey the Articles. Severe punishments were meeted out to offenders. Article XCI proclaimed that '... anyone pulling a knife in anger, to harm or to injure another person, shall be nailed to the mast with a knife through his hand, and shall remain standing there until he pulls his hand off ...'.

The ship's company – the bulk of those on board – was divided into three groups, referred to as watches, taking turns to man the ship. Tasks included keeping watch, taking the helm, cleaning the decks and pumping out the hold. A steady rhythm of alternate four-hour watches continued day in day out: six watches to the day. During free spells, there would be time for make and mend chores or for resting and sleeping. Changing the watch would be signalled by the drummer, whose beat marked the invariable regularity of life and work on board an East Indiaman. While the ship's company would often be a disparate collection of disorderly types, once on board they had to bow to the order and discipline required to keep the vessel running and afloat. Vigorous punishment of offenders and the monotonous regularity of existence on an East Indiaman left little room for the supposed free and easy life of a sailor. . . . . . . .

Portrait of a naval officer. The boatswain's whistle is suspended on a cord as an honorary symbol. Anonymous painting, c. 1600.

# Tragic loss of the Hollandia



The loss of a ship has always been the kind of dramatic event that appeals to the imagination. Naturally, this applies to the East Indiamen that disappeared as much as any other vessel. In fact, today the wrecks of East Indiamen offer the only material evidence of the former VOC fleet. While not one of all the ships that did not sink has been preserved, despite lying for hundreds of years on the seabed, it is the ships that sank and stranded that have withstood the ravages of time. Shipwrecks form a kind of time capsule: when a ship sinks the vessel ceases to function in an instant. And once it is on the seabed there is no chance of the remains being tampered with by human hand. Responsible archaeological research into various wrecks has produced a complete and coherent picture of the ships that served the Dutch East India Company. From that perspective, this tremendous interest in VOC wrecks (to date some thirty-three have been located) can be well appreciated: they provide a real contribution to current knowledge about the Company.

Ironically, this interest focuses on the failures of the VOC as a transport company. After all, a shipwreck represents a vessel's premature end: an attempt to sail from one place to another that did not succeed. A real danger exists, therefore, of losing sight of the fact that by far the majority of VOC ships plying between Europe and Asia reached their destinations without any problem. In the entire period of the Company's existence, less than three per cent of the total number of VOC ships sailing from Europe to Asia were lost, either through misfortune or enemy action. For homeward bound ships (Asia to Europe) the figure is less than five per cent. The years from 1721 to 1748 represented a relatively disastrous period for the VOC. In that space no less than 89 ships were lost. This was more than a third of all the VOC vessels ever shipwrecked (246) throughout the two centuries of the Company's existence.

One of the 89 was the *Hollandia*. On 3 July 1743 this ship sailed from the Texel roadstead on the start of the long voyage to Batavia. But the ship did not get far. Ten days later, on 13 July, the *Hollandia* went down off the Scilly Isles southwest of England. For some still unknown reason the master, Jan Kelder, had wandered off the prescribed course for the Channel. As a result, the ship found itself among the treacherous rocks of this British archipelago. The night was pitch black and visibility extremely poor. The ship scraped over a rock and, after having struggled along with a gashed hull, the *Hollandia* eventually sank to the bottom. The ships'

◀ Objects of silver tableware with the arms of the Van Imhoff and Bentinck families from the wreck of the Hollandia (sank in 1743).

Hendrik Frans van Imhoff and Mathilde Florentine Marie Bentinck. Both died in the wreck of the Hollandia in 1743. The portraits bear their respective arms which are also engraved on the silver tableware. Anonymous painter, first half eighteenth century; private collection.

maiden passage became its final voyage. The brand new East Indiaman had only just been delivered to the Amsterdam chamber. It was one in a series of 150-foot ships which had been designed, fitted out and equipped at Oostenburg – the VOC shipyard in Amsterdam – according to an entirely new standard.

Like every other shipwreck, the disappearance of the *Hollandia* represented a considerable loss of capital to the VOC. All the investments in the construction and equipage of the vessel were lost in a single moment when the vessel hit that fatal rock. The salvage operation, undertaken immediately after the disaster by Gerard Bolwerk, the VOC's man in London, with the assistance of the English diver John Lethbridge, made little headway. Because of the tremendous depths and the strong current at the site of the wreck, the work came to nothing. Moreover, beside the financial debacle, the demise of a ship was also a personal drama, the often incalculable suffering of the relatives of those who succumbed in the wreck.

The loss of the *Hollandia* cost the lives of all 276 hands on board. Only a few of their names are known. Among the passengers travelling on board the *Hollandia* was a prominent personage: Hendrik Frans van Imhoff, recently appointed senior merchant and the younger brother of Gustaaf Willem van Imhoff, then governor general in Batavia. Frans van Imhoff was accompanied by his wife Mathilde Florentine Marie Bentinck and her sister Anna, of a prominent Amsterdam patrician family.

Accompanying the couple was a large collection of tableware, including silver forks, knives and various types of spoon, as well as pewter candelabras. Some of these items of tableware bore the combined

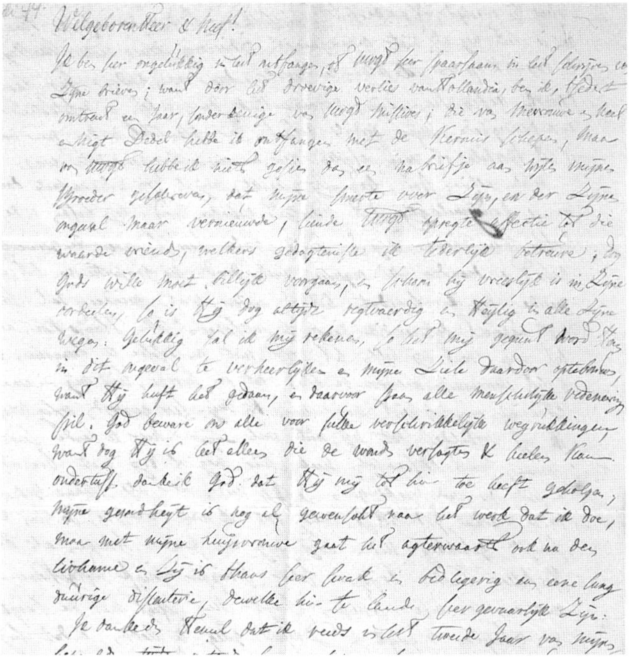

Extract from a letter from Gustaaf Willem Baron van Imhoff to his nephew J. Boreel Janszoon, fiscal advocate to the Amsterdam admiralty, 5 July 1744:

*Dear Sir and Nephew! I have been extremely unlucky in receiving, or your honour has been exceptionally sparing in sending letters, since with the sad loss of the Hollandia, I have been without any missive from your honour for one year; I received that from Mrs and nephew and niece Dedel with the Kermis (Fair) ships, but from your honour I saw nothing except a note addressed to my late brother, which, when I saw the integrity of your affection for those worthy friends, reopened the wounds of his and his companions' demise, the memory of which I tenderly cherish; yet God's will shall be done, and while He is terrible in His judgment, He is always just and Holy in His ways. I count myself lucky that I have been able to praise Him for this accident and so to sustain my soul, for it is He who has done this and in the face of this, all human rationalisation is confounded. May God spare us from all such bereavements, for only He can alleviate and heal the pain.*

In a passage steeped in humility, Van Imhoff tries to reconcile his sense of loss for his brother. Van Imhoff had eagerly anticipated the arrival of Hendrik Frans to the Indies. His death in the Hollandia disaster was a cause of great sadness.
Algemeen Rijksarchief, The Hague.

Gustaaf Willem Baron van Imhoff (1705-1750), Governor General (1743-1750). Van Imhoff's younger brother Hendrik and his wife died when the Hollandia went down in 1743.
Anonymus painting.

arms of the Bentinck and Van Imhoff families, symbolising the union of Frans and Mathilde. Shortly before leaving for Asia they had purchased the service from various craftsmen in Amsterdam.

Almost a year later Gustaaf Willem van Imhoff wrote in a letter to his nephew Jacob Boreel Janszoon, fiscal advocate to the Amsterdam admiralty: 'I have been extremely unlucky in receiving, or your honour has been exceptionally sparing in sending letters, since with the sad loss of the *Hollandia*, I have been without any missive from your honour for one year; I received that from Mrs and nephew and niece Dedel with the *Kermis* (Fair) ships, but from your honour I saw nothing except a note addressed to my late brother, which, when I saw the integrity of your affection for those worthy friends, reopened the wounds of his and his companions' demise, the memory of which I tenderly cherish; yet God's will shall be done, and while He is terrible in His judgment, He is always just and Holy in His ways. I count myself lucky that I have been able to praise Him for this accident and so to sustain my soul, for it is He who has done this and in the face of this, all human rationalisation is confounded.' The humility of the letter barely conceals the sadness of the Governor General at the loss of his brother and his companions, whose arrival he had so eagerly anticipated.

Hendrik Frans van Imhoff, Mathilde Florentine Marie Bentinck and her sister Anna – their memory was tenderly cherished. How the memories of the other victims of the *Hollandia* disaster were preserved remains unknown: their deaths are commemorated in the grave of the unknown sailor.

# New hosepipe fire extinguisher

It takes only a little imagination to see that travelling to the Orient three centuries ago was not unlike a journey into space today. The long voyage brought the Dutch East India Company ships to distant, unknown places. It was a perilous undertaking involving enormous financial resources. Reason enough for the directors of the Company, the Heren XVII, to set high standards for the construction and equipment of their ships. For several items the VOC depended on manufacturers who produced high-quality technical apparatus.

The fire extinguishers carried on board East Indiamen are a good example of the type of high tech produced in the Dutch Republic in the seventeenth and eighteenth centuries. In 1687 the Heren XVII decided that these should be standard equipment on the Company's ships. The favoured model was one that fire fighters in general recognised as the most advanced type: the hosepipe fire extinguisher. This machine had been developed in the 1670s by Jan van der Heyden together with his brother Nicolaes.

Surely one of the most intriguing figures to emerge from the Dutch Golden Age: Jan van der Heyden was a man of many talents, in fact something of a Dutch *homo universalis*. He was a creditable painter – especially of views of Amsterdam – and possessed a tremendous capacity for organisation: as an employee in the city's civil service he ran the streetlight department and the fire brigade. Moreover, as an engineer *avant la lettre* he produced a number of crucial inventions. Perhaps the most important of these was the hosepipe fire extinguisher.

The most obvious improvement on existing fire extinguishers was the use of a hosepipe to transport the water – not just from the source to the machine, but at the firefighting end of the extinguisher too. Van der Heyden's apparatus incorporated a suction pump mechanism with a pressure tank to ensure an uninterrupted jet of water. Here again the 'newly invented, hosepipe fire extinguisher' differed from the models that had preceded it, as the patent for the invention clearly articulates: 'Hosepipe fire extinguishers, featuring a continuous jet to spout at the fire with a flexible hose attached, referred to because of its shape as a snake ...'. With the 'snake' it was now possible to reach the fire's centre. It featured a leather hosepipe reinforced inside with brass rings so that the pipe remained flexible while ensuring that the pump's suction power could not be cut.

In addition to being an inventor, Jan van der Heyden was also an astute entre-

◀ Parts of the hosepipe fire extinguisher recovered from the wreck of the Hollandia (sank in 1743). Brass screw attachments to link the separate hoses to the pipes. These connections were cast in moulds so that all standard screw attachments would fit each other.

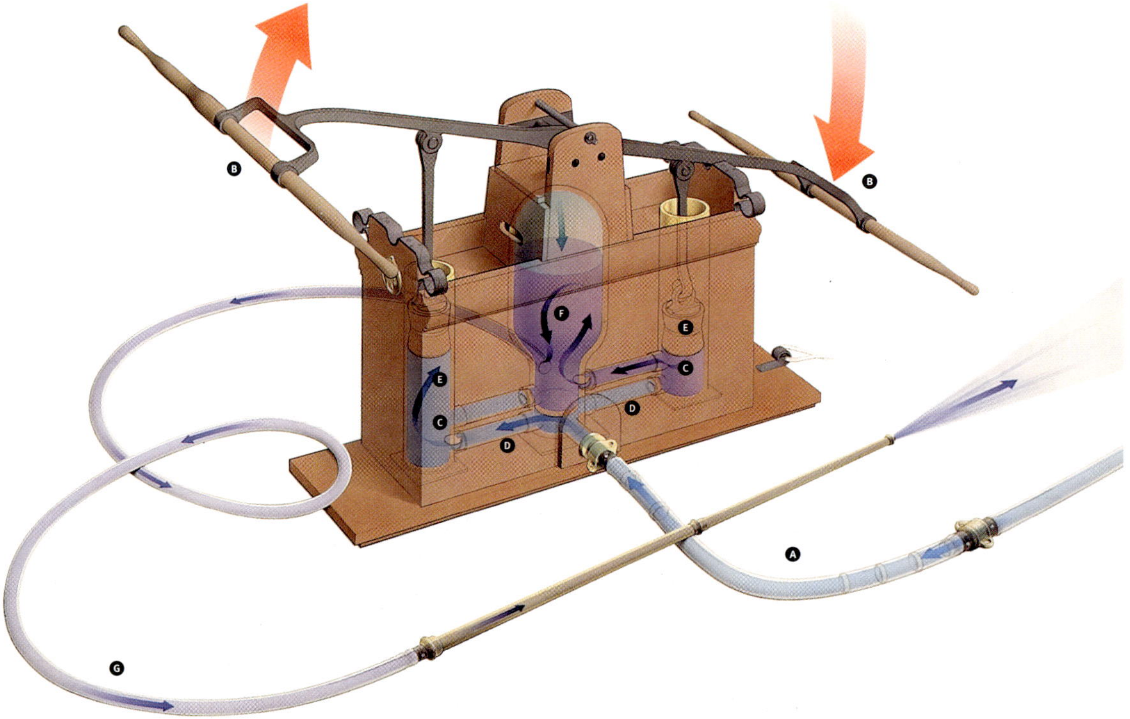


Reconstruction of a hosepipe fire extinguisher. The suction pipe (A) hangs in the water or in a basin filled by with buckets of water. By operating the levers (B) up and down the water is pumped into the cylinders (C). Valves (D) stop the water flowing back. When the lever on one side is up, the piston (E) in the other cylinder is down, expelling the water from the pressure tank (F). Because of the excess pressure the water leaves the machine through the hose (G) and the spout. Drawing by Paul Maas, 1995.

preneur who succeeded in promoting his product in an inventive way. In 1690 he published *Beschryving der nieuwelijks uitgevonden en ge-octrojeerde Slang-Brand-Spuiten* (Description of the newly invented and patented Hosepipe Fire Extinguishers). It listed an array of statistics to prove the enormous advantage of the hosepipe fire extinguisher. Moreover, the volume contained a series of prints made by the inventor himself. Here Van der Heyden put his training as an artist to good use. Not only was he able to produce clear technical drawings, Van der Heyden's etchings also showed evocative scenes in which his machine demonstrated its usefulness. And in addition to the *Beschryving* Jan Van der Heyden produced a continuous flow of advertising flyers with Dutch and French texts. His Amsterdam firm aimed at an international market.

But back on board the East Indiaman, this machine would not only be useful when fire broke out, it was also a handy apparatus for cleaning the decks. Moreover, it could be used for wetting the sails – when wet the canvas was less porous and therefore caught the wind more effectively. Finally, the apparatus served as a pump to extract water; the hosepipe pump could shift five or six times as much as an ordinary ship's pump.

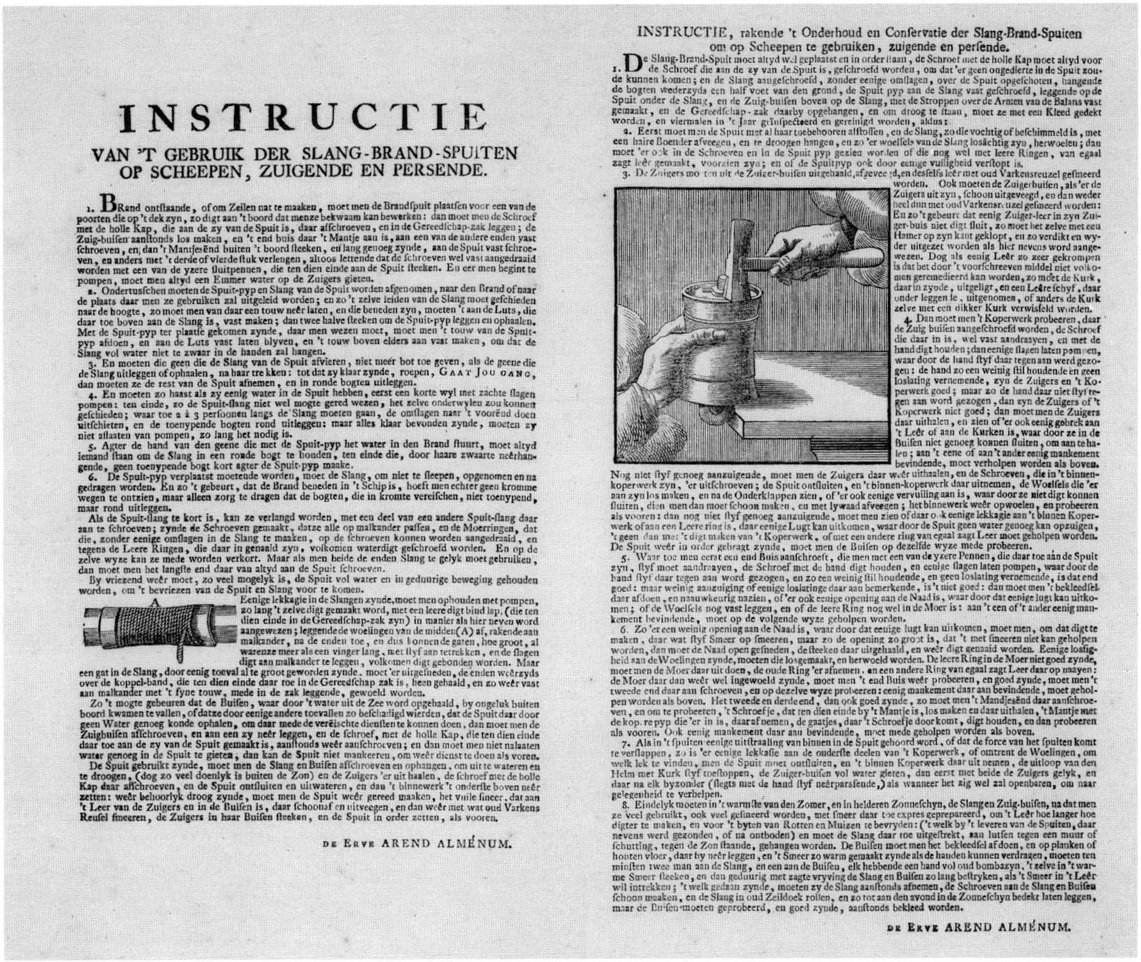


Manual with instructions for maintenance of ships fire extinguishers by fire extinguisher manufacturer Alménum, final quarter eighteenth century.

**A** East Indiaman, the *Swarte Leeuw*, moored off Oostenburg shipyard in Amsterdam in 1690. The illustration reveals the situation after fire had ravaged the ship. On the left is the shipyard's fire extinguisher; on the right in the foreground is a fire extinguisher from one of the harbour districts. Engraving by Jan van der Heyden from *Beschijving der nieuwlijks uitgevonden en geoctroyeerde Slang-brand-spuiten tegenwoordig binnen Amsterdam in gebruik zijnde* (Amsterdam 1690).

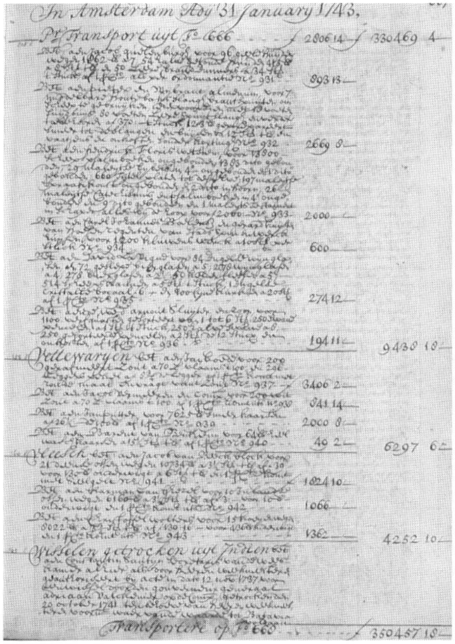

Fragments of Van der Heyden's fire extinguisher have been recovered from the wreck of the East Indiaman *Hollandia* (1743), although little remains of the apparatus as a whole. Yet these individual parts represent an important aspect of the manufacture of the hosepipe fire extinguisher. The spouts and the hose connections have screw attachments. These links were cast in standard moulds so that every hose would fit every machine. Van der Heyden referred to this feature in the extensive instructions that accompanied the invention: 'If the hose is too short it can be extended by attaching part of another hose; the screws have been made so that each fits the other'. In short, the parts were interchangeable and the correct spares could be delivered if a machine needed repairs. This is an important clue to the success of the apparatus, which remained in use until the late nineteenth century.

Archaeological finds recovered from the *Hollandia* reveal the extensive regularisation and standardisation in production methods that the Van der Heyden brothers achieved in their fire extinguisher factory. They represent one of the first modern Dutch enterprises of the proto-industrial age.

◀ Journal of the senior bookkeeper of the Amsterdam chamber of the voc, 31 January 1743:

*Paid to Pieter and Wijbrant Alménum for 7 medium-sized wooden-tank hosepipe fire extinguishers for use on board ship, each with 18 feet of suction pipe, 80 feet of leather hose and other fittings at f370.- a piece, 123 lb prepared grease for the hoses and pipes at 12 stuivers a pound and casks and expenses, without discount no. 923 f2669.- and 8 stuivers.*

Pieter and Wijbrant Alménum, who took over the fire extinguisher factory from Van der Heyden, supplied 7 extinguishers to the voc. Each machine had six metres of suction hose and 25 metres for spouting, and a supply of grease to maintain the leather hoses. Algemeen Rijksarchief, The Hague.

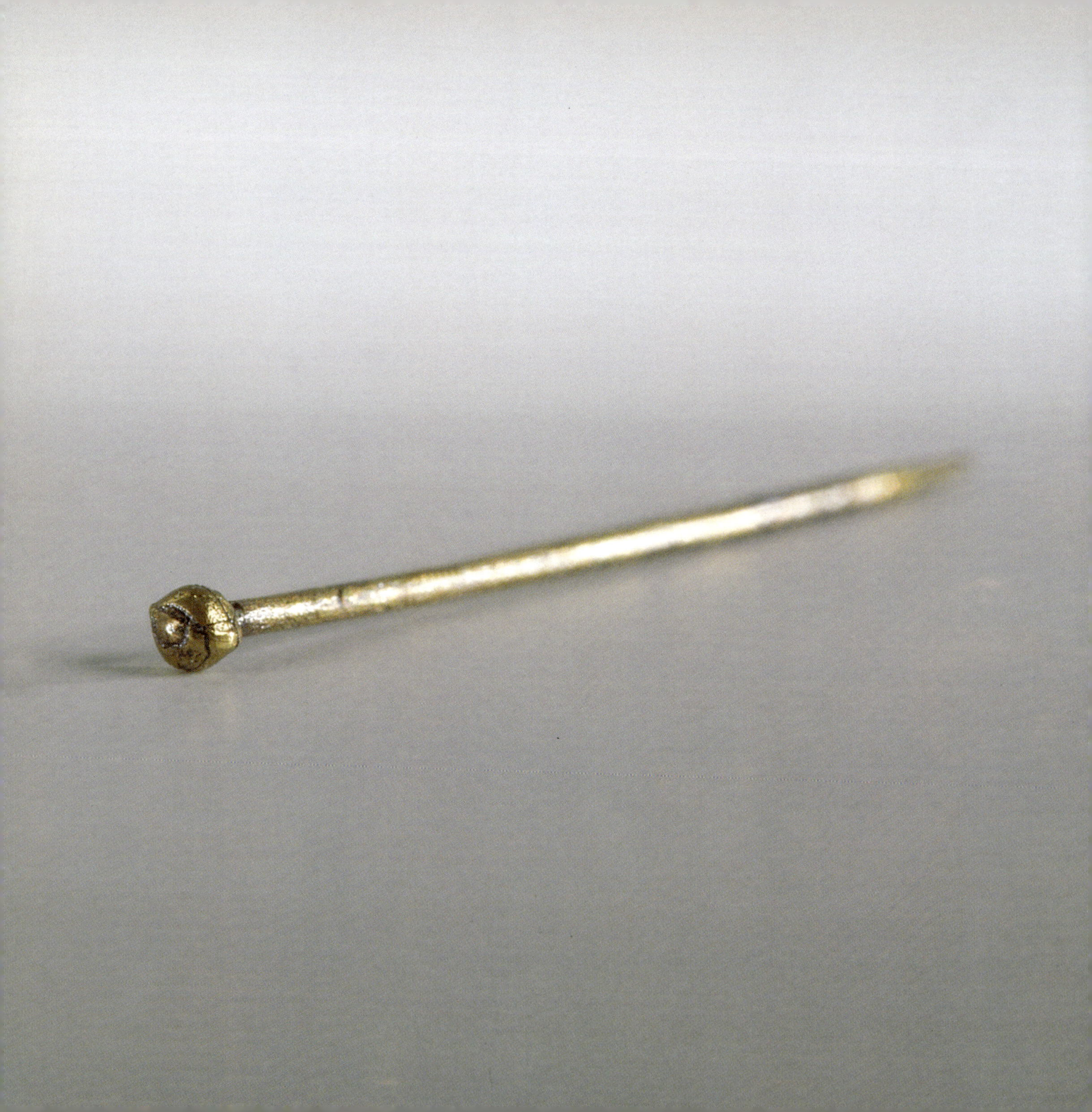

# Significance of a pin

It is not perhaps the most spectacular of finds, the collection of pins from the wreck of the *Amsterdam*: at first sight a pin is a rather mundane and everyday kind of object. Yet the eighteenth-century pin is remarkably interesting, especially the production process with which that modest item was made. This was the conclusion reached by Adam Smith (1723-1790), the Scottish Enlightenment theorist who is considered to have been one of the founders of the modern science of economics.

Smith made his name with a sizeable tome that appeared in 1776 entitled *An Inquiry into the Nature and Causes of the Wealth of Nations*. In this systematic and comprehensive study of the problems of economics, Smith focussed in the first few pages on the pin. Here too, the author is forced to admit that the pin is a relatively unimpressive artifact. But this does not detract from the fact that the eighteenth-century manufacture of pins provided a splendid example of a branch of industry in which the division of labour had been employed to a significant degree.

In the very first sentence of the first chapter of his *Wealth of Nations* Smith noted that 'The greatest improvement in the productive powers of labour ... seem to have been the effects of the division of labour.' And to illustrate the point a description is given of the procedures followed in the pin factory. If a single worker were to carry out all the steps involved in the production of a pin, Smith argued, he would only be able to produce a maximum of twenty pins a day. By dividing the procedure into different tasks and employing ten workers in a factory to perform the various successive steps in the manufacture of a pin, he calculated that the production per worker could increase to 4,800 pins a day. Profits would sky-rocket.

Manufacture of pins in the eighteenth century followed a series of stages involving a number of specialised workers. Smith offered a brief description of the production process: 'One man draws out the wire, another straights it, a third cuts it, a fourth points it, a fifth grinds it at the top for receiving the head; to make the head requires two or three distinct operations; to put it on is a peculiar business, to whiten the pins is another; ...'

This production process is also described in another significant work which, like Smith's *Wealth of Nations*, is something of a monument of eighteenth-century Enlightenment philosophy: the *Encyclopédie des Arts et Métiers*, which appeared in several volumes from 1751. The ambitious objective of the compilers Diderot and

Pin found in the wreck of the Amsterdam (sank in 1749), copper. Stichting voc-schip Amsterdam, Amsterdam.

Reconstruction of a pin as found in the wreck of the Amsterdam (sank in 1749). The head of the pin is made of a piece of copper wire twisted into a minute spiral. Drawing by Eric van Rootselaar, 1995.

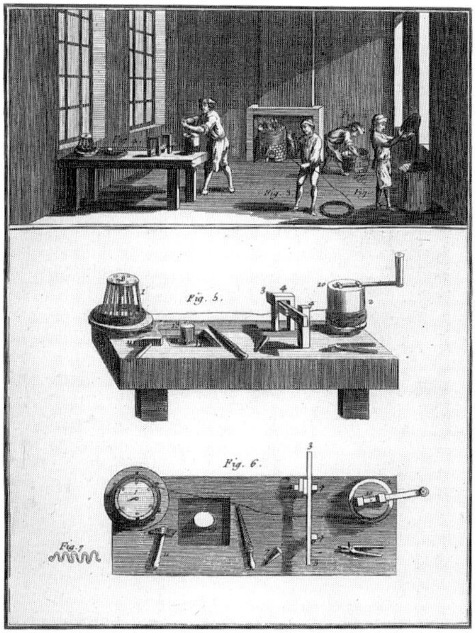

Plate I

Plate II

d'Alembert was to compile a survey of all useful knowledge. Part 4 deals with various branches of industry. It includes data that the compilers gathered from artisans about the practice of their craft. The descriptions are illustrated with numerous engravings of workshops and tools, providing an excellent overview of the state of technology in the eighteenth century. The result is a work which reveals the world of industry as it was at the eve of the Industrial Revolution.

Three engravings in the *Encyclopédie* (of which two are separate pictures of tools) provide an illustrated description of the various tasks of the *épinglier* (pinmaker). Figure 4 in plate I shows a man drawing the copper wire through the aperture to obtain the required thickness. The wire is wound onto a reel and subsequently, in figure 2 of plate II, unwound and straightened. On the floor beside the man whose job this is are the straightened pieces of copper wire. Bundles of copper wire would then be cut into pin-length pieces by the men shown seated on the floor (figures 3 and 4, plate II). With the aid of an apparatus attached to the thigh (figures 21 and

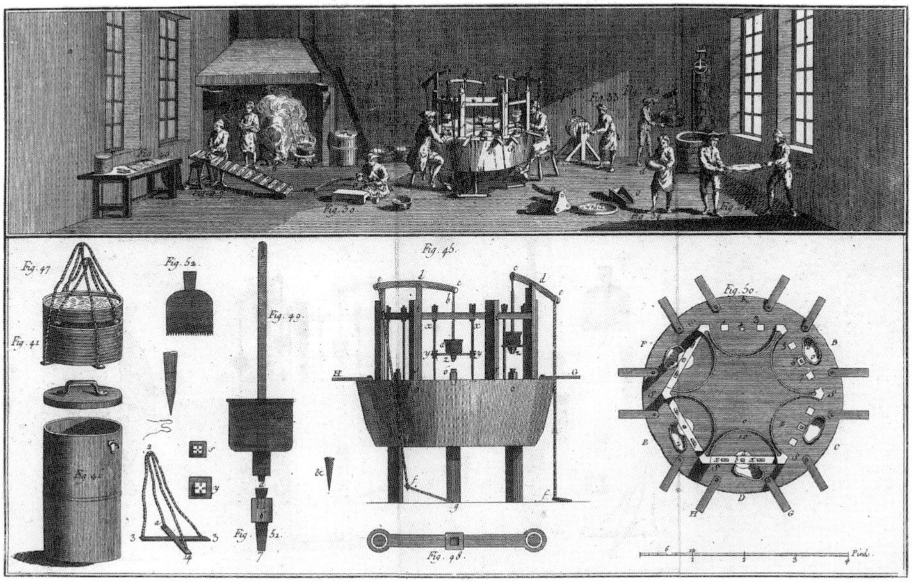

Plate III

◀ Eighteenth-century pin factory and the tools used by pinmakers for the various stages of the production process.

Engraving from Diderot and d'Alambert, *Encyclopédie des Arts et des Métiers*.

22, plate II) each man was able to produce 4,200 pieces per hour. Each of these would be sharpened at one end on a grinder turned with a wheel (figures 5 to 8, plate II).

The head was then attached to the pin. This was made of a piece of copper wire wound into a minuscule spiral. Using a weight and a tiny anvil the spiral, having been heated and cooled to the correct temperature, would be beaten onto the end of the pin into a knob. The machine for this purpose was powered with a pedal and could accommodate more than one worker (figure 12, 13 and 18, plate III). An enlarged picture of the pins from the *Amsterdam* reveals the contours of the twisted copper wire that formed the head of the pin. A subject that might at first have seemed futile and unimportant appears on closer inspection to be the product of a complex and highly significant sector of the industrial world of the eighteenth century. This tiny detail of the Dutch East India Company's history reveals how modern production methods had already begun to make their entrance in the pre-industrial age.

# Silver for export



The Dutch East India Company was primarily an import concern. In other words, the focus of the Company's activities lay in the supply and sale of Asiatic products on the European market. In the overall context of the VOC's trade relations, the export of European goods to Asia was a marginal factor; there was simply no real demand for European products in the Asian market. This is more than apparent from the registers of cargos of VOC fleets sailing from Europe to the East Indies. Most of the items in the holds of vessels leaving for Asia were materials required for the various overseas factories of the Company, bricks and cannons for the forts, as well as anchors for the VOC fleet in Asia. These materials ensured that, despite the absence of trade goods, vessels would carry sufficient weight for the necessary draught.

In fact, the value of this type of cargo was more than surpassed by that of the supply of precious metals which almost every outward-bound East Indiaman carried. This could amount to as much as 400,000 guilders worth of coin or specie – minted or unminted silver or gold. As a

◀ Silver bars in a chest, found in the wreck of the East Indiaman Slot ter Hoge (sank in 1724). The ingots are stamped with the mark of the Zeeland chamber of the VOC and with an unidentified assayer's mark in the form of a rosette. The Slot ter Hooge carried fifteen chests of silver: the total value of the bullion on board the ship was 350,000 guilders.

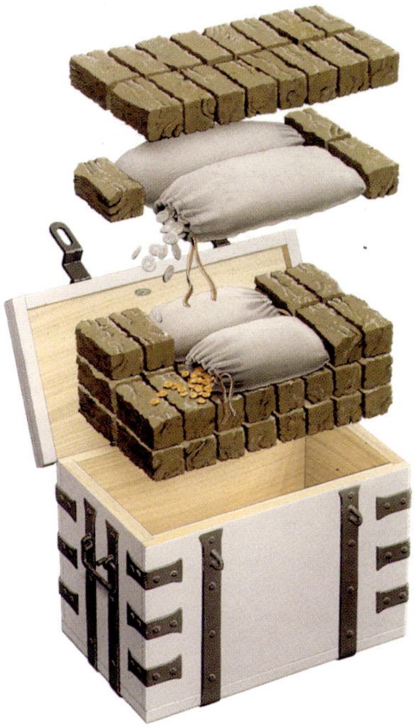

▶ Reconstruction of a chest with silver as found in the wreck of the East Indiaman Slot ter Hoge (sank in 1724). The chests were made of thick pine planks reinforced with iron fittings and two locks. The money bags were made of canvas and tied with a single lace. Peat was placed in the spaces between the bags and the walls of the chest to prevent damage in the months at sea. Drawing by Eric van Rootselaar, 1995.

Journal of the senior bookkeeper of the Amsterdam chamber of the VOC, 30 June 1743:

*Specie for the Indies from the Rotterdam chamber Gls: 100021: 5: which amount from the account of the chamber to the skipper Christiaan de Jongh and mate Pieter Oostendorp of the ship Ruyven 8 chests containing 483 bars of silver of 8 marks each, in total 3,864 marks at 11 pennings 20 grain 3,810 marks and 4 pennings at f 26/4 marked Fine the same to be delivered to the Governor General or deputy at Batavia by bill of lading to the Liasse 79 no 24 f100021 51*

This extract from the bookkeeper's journal provides an idea of the amount of silver being sent to Asia by the VOC. Silver ingots valued at more than 100,000 guilders were bought for a ship of the Rotterdam chamber. Algemeen Rijksarchief, The Hague.

828 In Amsterdam Adij 30 Juny 1743.

Pr Transport uijt Fo 827 ... 38460

42 818

Specien voor Indien aande Kamer van Rotterdam Gls 100021 5 ... 100021 5

Adij 31 July 1743,

De Ontfangers aande naargenoemde Gls 151884 2

Transportere op Fo 829 ... 11887

transporter of bullion the Company developed in the course of its history into an export enterprise. In all, the VOC shipped around 150 million guilders worth of silver ingots to Asia: around one-and-a-half million kilograms of pure silver.

To focus on silver in particular, this was exported to Asia in the form of semi-manufactured bars. Silver ingots were first sent to the East in 1620 as an experiment. After 1646 the VOC sent the metal more frequently, although often with gaps of several years. In the 1680s silver ingots became a regular part of every consignment of bullion to Asia.

The enormous increase in silver exports accompanied the gradual structural change in trading patterns between Europe and Asia that took place towards the end of the seventeenth century. While originally the VOC was able to employ the profits from trade and transport between various areas in Asia – the so-called inter-Asian trade – to buy Asian products for the European market, in the 1680s it was becoming clear that these earnings from local trade in Asia were insufficient to meet the demands of the growing European market. Demand was increasing for textiles from regions such as Bengal, where the means of exchange were precious metals, especially silver. To ensure supply, bullion had to be imported from Europe. Meanwhile, the eighteenth century also witnessed a major increase in the import of Chinese tea. And this was also paid for in silver.

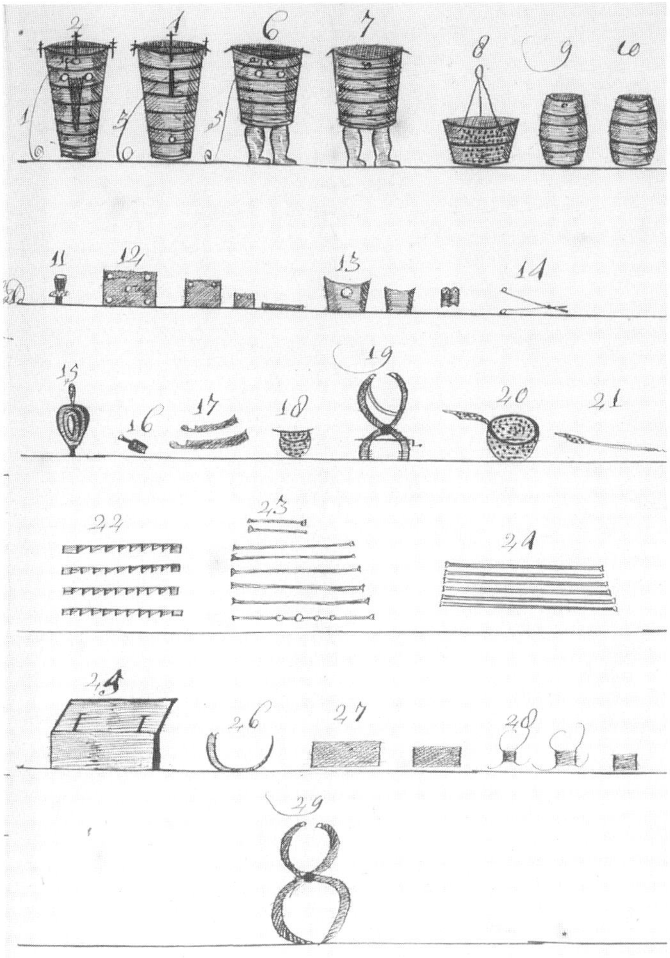

◀ Equipment of the English diver John Lethbridge of around 1730. The tools give an idea of the way he went about retrieving the bullion. Shown here are a money scoop (No. 16), a pair of tongs to lift money chests (No. 19), a 'net to fish for loose money' (No. 20) and various saws (No. 22). Lethbridge's wooden diving machine is also shown (Nos 2, 4, 6 and 7).
Algemeen Rijksarchief, The Hague.

Real de a ocho (Rial of eight), minted in Mexico in 1735. Many of these Spanish coins were melted down in Amsterdam and the metal shaped into silver bars. These ingots were then exported by the voc to Asia where the silver was used to strike coins of the local currencies.

A significant change occurred in the late seventeenth century, when Japan halted the plentiful and inexpensive supply of precious metal from which the Company had profited. In 1668 the Japanese authorities prohibited the export of silver. Exports of Japanese precious metals had previously reached one-and-a-half million guilders a year. This loss was a major blow to the voc's Asian operation which now no longer had the flexibility to finance the local trade independently. For the supply of specie Batavia was increasingly dependent on Europe.

Every year the governor general and the East Indies Council drew up a list of the required amount of funds known as the *Eis van Indien*. This was sent to the Republic, where the Heren XVII would examine and assess to what extent they were able to meet the requirements outlined in the *Eis*. The various chambers of the Company would then purchase the silver in proportion to a fixed ratio and send this to Asia. Silver could be bought through the flourishing precious metals market in Amsterdam. It was supplied by the annual silver fleet that came from the Spanish port of Cadiz loaded with Spanish *reales de a ocho*. This minted silver came from Spain's colonies of Mexico and Peru. Once acquired by the voc, these coins were

melted down and the silver transformed into bars. And reduced to the state of raw material, the silver could be reshaped in Asia into the local coinage that the voc needed to be able to buy produce at competitive prices. Because the silver content of the Spanish reals was less than that of the various Asian coins, an assayer was often needed before the silver even left the Republic, to ensure that the metal had the required level of purity for the Asian market.

The ingots of silver were packed in chests. A receipt would be signed by the master listing in detail the content and value of each chest. All the silver would be stored in the captain's cabin. Once in Batavia the master would hand the bullion over to the employees of the Company treasury. From there it was distributed throughout the various factories in Asia. In the eighteenth century Bengal absorbed the main portion of the silver sent to Batavia, sometimes more than half. It was inefficient to pay in coins other than local currency. So local rupees were struck from the supply of silver. The VOC was able to ensure that this could be achieved without intervention from Indian bankers and under their own supervisor.

As a result, the Company became an important link in the global transfer of silver from the rich mines in America, through Europe, to Asia. In the later seventeenth century the movement of silver formed a vital part of the trade pattern that the VOC maintained. Only rarely did this go wrong. The loss of an outward-bound East Indiaman represented an incidental but expensive interruption to the flow of funds. Shipwrecks were often followed by intense efforts to salvage the cargo. For example, in the case of the *Slot ter Hooge*, an East Indiaman from the Zeeland chamber that sank in 1724 off the coast of Madeira. On board was an enormous amount of bullion with a total value of some 350,000 guilders, including fifteen boxes of silver bars. Almost immediately after the *Slot ter Hooge* sank the governors of the Zeeland chamber organised a salvage operation led by John Lethbridge. This famous English diver had invented a diving machine in 1715. It was a watertight barrel with a crystal window and two openings with leather sleeves for a person's arms. With this apparatus Lethbridge managed to recover as much as ninety per cent of the treasure from the seabed. The remains that were left behind underwater included one of the boxes of silver. Almost two-and-half centuries later, this was lifted by the Belgian diver Robert Sténuit and eventually transferred to the Rijksmuseum.

# Importing porcelain

How the Dutch East India Company's involvement in the export of Chinese porcelain to Europe developed is revealing. During the first stormy years of its existence, the Company forced its way into the market by seizing a number of Portuguese ships – carracks – carrying porcelain. Despite the powerful position the VOC later acquired in Asia, the Company was unable to enter regular, direct trade in Chinese ports. However, through Chinese intermediaries it was possible to have the required products, such as silk, tea, drugs and porcelain shipped to Formosa (Taiwan), where the VOC maintained a trading post. When this was abandoned in 1662, the need for direct contact with mainland China again became apparent. Ambassadors were sent to the Imperial court in Peking to obtain concessions from the Chinese authorities; but this expensive enterprise bore practically no fruit.

Towards the close of the seventeenth century a steady stream of Chinese junks began to reach Batavia, by then the principal entrepôt of the inter-Asian trade network. From Batavia the Company was able to supply the European market with Chinese wares. Yet this was a rather unsatisfactory method of obtaining the required products. This became all the more obvious in the years 1718 and 1722, when the flow of Chinese junks suddenly stagnated due to a ban on exports by the Chinese authorities. Once again the directors of the Company found themselves in a vulnerable position and a new demand was raised for direct trade with China in VOC ships.

In 1729 a new initiative was taken. Without consulting the High Council in Batavia – they had given little heed to the entreaties of the Heren XVII on this point – direct trade between the Republic and the major export harbour of Canton was organised. Five years later it was decreed that ships bound for China should first stop at Batavia after all; but from Canton the homeward bound ships would sail direct to the Republic.

At last, in 1734, the VOC had achieved satisfactory terms on which to continue trading with China. In principle the Company wanted to keep as much of the purchase and transport of products in their own hands as possible. From the South China Sea the VOC ships sailed up the Pearl river to Whampoa roadstead. Here the ships anchored until they were loaded. VOC representatives (supercargas), who were responsible for purchasing products, would sail to Canton itself in small boats and hire a factory for the length of their stay. It was then essential to get down to

◀ Cornelis Pronk made a number of drawings in 1735 as models for Chinese porcelain manufacturers. This design shows three doctors. The Amsterdam painter and draughtsman's contract with the Heren XVII stipulated that he would spend three years working on drawing designs and models for various porcelain wares. Copies of his drawings were sent via Batavia to the Chinese commercial centre of Canton. Drawing by Cornelis Pronk, 1735.

Resolutions of the Heren XVII, 10 October 1749:

*Porcelain as much as required for the bottom layer, underneath Boullon bowls with lids and dishes, all oval as in the drawing in duplicate, above 125 S, that is one hundred and twenty-five pieces, comprising 50 pieces red, blue and gold eye, the blue should be the least prominent colour, 50 white and blue, 25 enamelled.*

The VOC merchants in Canton bought with shopping lists from the Heren XVII – the Eis van Retour. These contained descriptions of the sort of porcelain required and the decorations on the various pieces. Also listed was the number of each item to be ordered. Originally drawn up by the Heren XVII in person, after 1756 the Eis was compiled by a committee specially concerned with the China trade. Algemeen Rijksarchief, The Hague.

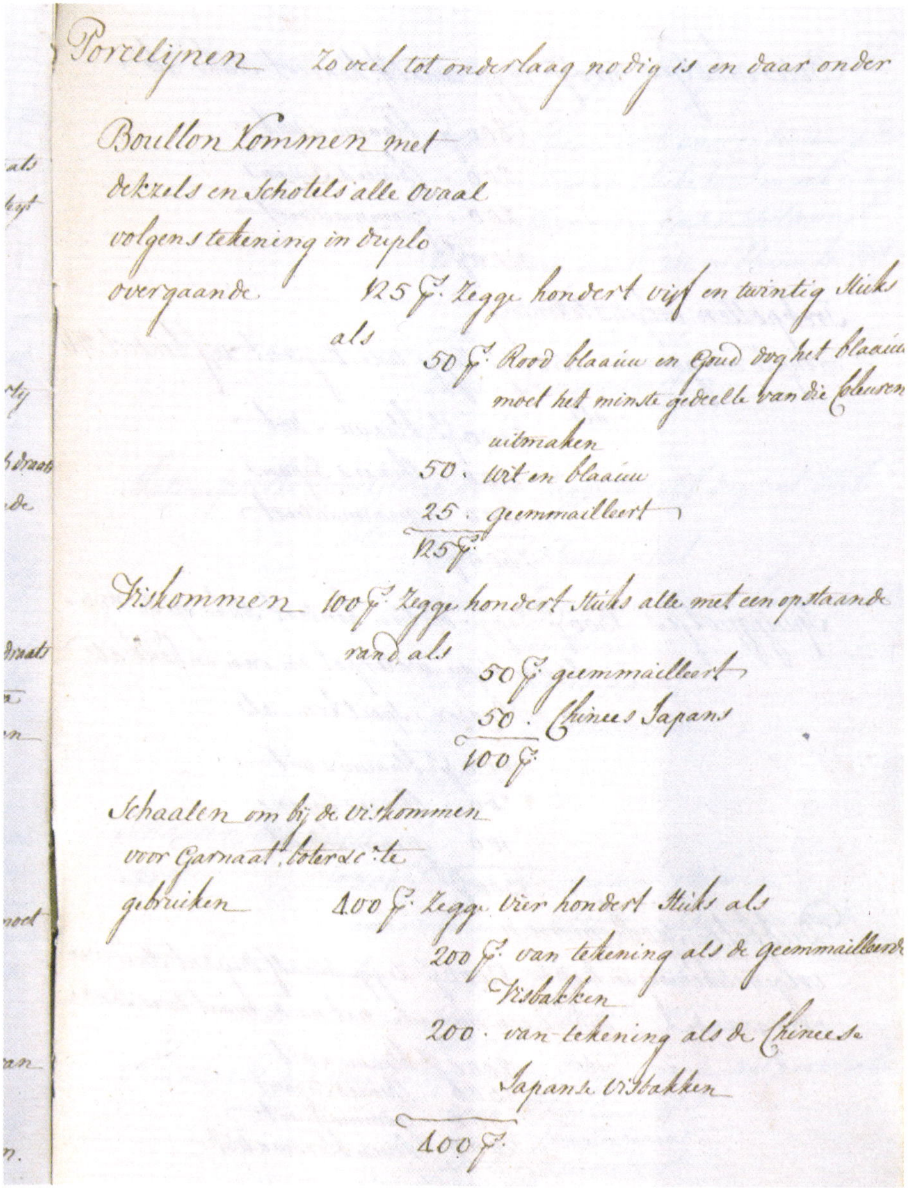
Porcelynen Zo veel tot onderlaag nodig is en daar onder
Boullon Kommen met
dekzels en Schotels alle Ovaal
volgens tekening in Duplo
overgaande 125 S: Zegge hondert vijf en twintig Stuks
als
50 S: Rood blaauw en Goud oog het blaauw
moet het minste gedeelte van die Couleuren
uitmaken
50. Wit en blaauw
25. geemmailleert
125 S:
Viskommen 100 S: Zegge hondert Stuks alle met een opstaande
rand als
50 S: geemmailleert
50. Chinees Japans
100 S:
Schaalen om bij de Viskommen
voor Garnaat, boter &c: te
gebruiken 400 S: Zegge vier hondert Stuks als
200 S: van tekening als de geemmailleerde
Visbakken
200. van tekening als de Chinees
Japanse Visbakken
400 S:

business as soon as possible, to buy the required wares and to be able to start the return voyage at the beginning of the northern monsoon season. Of the various items available in Canton, the most important was tea. The heavy porcelain provided an ideal compensation for the light tea: a layer of porcelain ware underneath in the hold gave the ship the required draught.

In practice, the purchase of porcelain was anything but simple; it made enormous demands on the organisational resources of the VOC. The supercargas were given lists with precise instructions concerning the kinds of porcelain they had to buy and the motifs with which these should be decorated. Also stipulated was the required number of each type. An *Eis van Retour* was a kind of shopping list drawn up in the Republic, originally by the various VOC chambers separately, but after 1734 by the Heren XVII. In 1756 the task was delegated to a special committee in charge of trade with China: the *Chinasche Commissie*.

Purchasing traditional types of porcelain did not generally present problems. There was a supply available in the Cantonese porcelain shops which the supercargas visited immediately upon arrival. For the larger pieces, including table services,

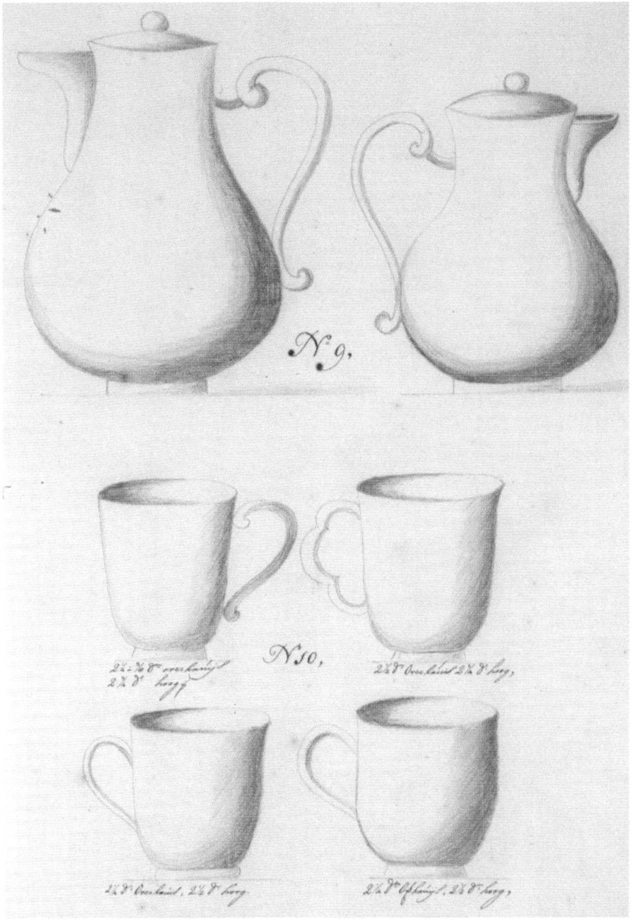


**A** Model drawings of porcelain milk jugs and chocolate cups, appended to the Eis van Retour that went to Canton in 1756. The factory in Canton received new drawing like these each year. They were diagrams for the Chinese merchants to illustrate the kind of porcelain ware that the VOC wanted to buy. Algemeen Rijksarchief, The Hague.

for example, separate orders or commissions would be placed. This would involve a contract with a Chinese merchant in which the latter would undertake to deliver a fixed amount of porcelain for a certain price and within a given period. It was the Chinese merchant's task to commission a porcelain manufacturer to produce the products. To ensure that the correct order was made, the VOC supplied the supercargas with examples. These might be made of wood, but sometimes also of

Porcelain pattern plate, c. 1790/1795. This plate has decorations around the rim and monogram cartouches which served as examples for the Chinese potters.

earthenware, specially made for the VOC in potters in Delft.

In the early eighteenth century the tastes of the VOC's European customers began to change. Besides the mass products imported by the Company, a more exclusive demand emerged for Chinese porcelain decorated with European motifs. To meet this specifically European demand, in 1734 the Heren XVII made an arrangement with Cornelis Pronk, a well-known artist in Amsterdam. In a period of three years Pronk produced one design a year. This was not just the decorative motif; it included drawings for each individual piece. Moreover, Pronk delivered the whole series to the Company with five copies. Costs of the production were borne by the client. Pronk's annual fee was 1,200 guilders.

Both parties kept to the contract. And Pronk's designs travelled to the other side of the world: through Batavia and Canton they eventually found their way to Ch'ing-tê Chê in the province of Kiangsi, traditionally the principal centre of pottery in China. There the drawings served as examples for the Chinese craftsmen.

This experiment with Pronk's designs was unique. It was the first long-term investment by the VOC in the porcelain trade. And this investment was not simply a response to existing demand; the directors were in fact aiming to influence the market. Because of the extent of specialisation involved in the purchasing of porcelain, the Company was able to match supply and demand with considerable accuracy within the limited confines of the trade contacts with China. Between European taste and Chinese industry lay a world of difference that the VOC managed to bridge, a successful venture reflected in the objects of Chinese porcelain. . . . . . . .

# Importing textiles

Towards the end of the seventeenth century a major shift occurred in the trading patterns of the Dutch East India Company. From around 1670 the directors of the Company began investing heavily in expanding the capacity of the VOC fleet, in the ships that sailed between Europe and Asia. A significant growth in the selection of goods purchased and shipped back to the Republic made this essential. Besides the traditional spices, relatively new products such as tea, coffee, saltpetre and porcelain were being introduced onto the European market on a large scale. Textile from India was one of the new products that was growing in significance for the VOC's intercontinental trade around 1700.

It would be inaccurate to suggest that the VOC's involvement in Indian textiles had been insignificant before this period. On the contrary, the purchase of cotton and linen played a considerable part in the local inter-Asian commercial network that the Company maintained in the early decades of its existence. Already, in 1603 the Heren XVII dictated a memorandum about trade in Indian textiles with a review of the required designs. The VOC was aiming at the large demand for textiles in Indochina and the Indonesian archipelago. Spices were shipped from the Moluccas and exchanged in the Indian textile centres (Gujarat in the northwest, Coromandel in the southwest, and Bengal in the northeast) for cotton fabrics. These materials were then shipped and sold throughout Southeast Asia.

The VOC's inter-Asian trade continued until well into the eighteenth century. But in the 1670s imports of textiles from India to the Republic started to become increasingly significant. It was the English and French East India Companies that paved the way in this trade, although eventually, with its enormous resources of capital, the Dutch Company was to become the largest European importer of textiles.

Foremost among these fabrics was printed cotton, or chintz. The designs were applied to the textile using a kind of batik method: a combination of dying – with the remainder of the cloth being covered with wax – and staining – the colours being applied to the fibres of the cloth with metal salts. In late seventeenth-century Europe, when chintz began to arrive in large quantities, this technique was still completely new. While the demand for chintz grew, stimulated by changes in fashion, supplies were entirely dependent on the Indian textile industry. But this was where the VOC's strength lay: an intercontinental company operating as an intermediary between Asia and Europe.

◄ Chintz sample from Coromandel (south-eastern coast of India). This sample was auctioned at the house of the merchant Abraham Ruurds of Leeuwarden in February 1783. The fabric bears the VOC monogram.

Resolutions of the Heren XVII, 6 October 1756:

*Bengal.*
*300 Ps Doereas Fine Decca diamond length 40 width 2 1/4 cob[icen]. These must be of extra fine quality, and the Netel cloth not too compact, so that the diamonds are shown at their best.*
*3/4 of the batch must be diamond pattern, as enclosed sample with ordinary dacca: 1/4 alternate diamonds all correctly made.*

Each year a list of requirements, or Eis van Retour, was compiled by the Heren XVII and sent to the Company's Asian trading posts. The Eis for 1757 and 1758 included a request for diamond-pattern fabric from Bengal. A piece of cloth was attached to the document as an example. The term Doereas indicates that the cloth was either diamond patterned or striped. Decca (today's Dacca) is either where the cloth was made or stored. Algemeen Rijksarchief, The Hague.

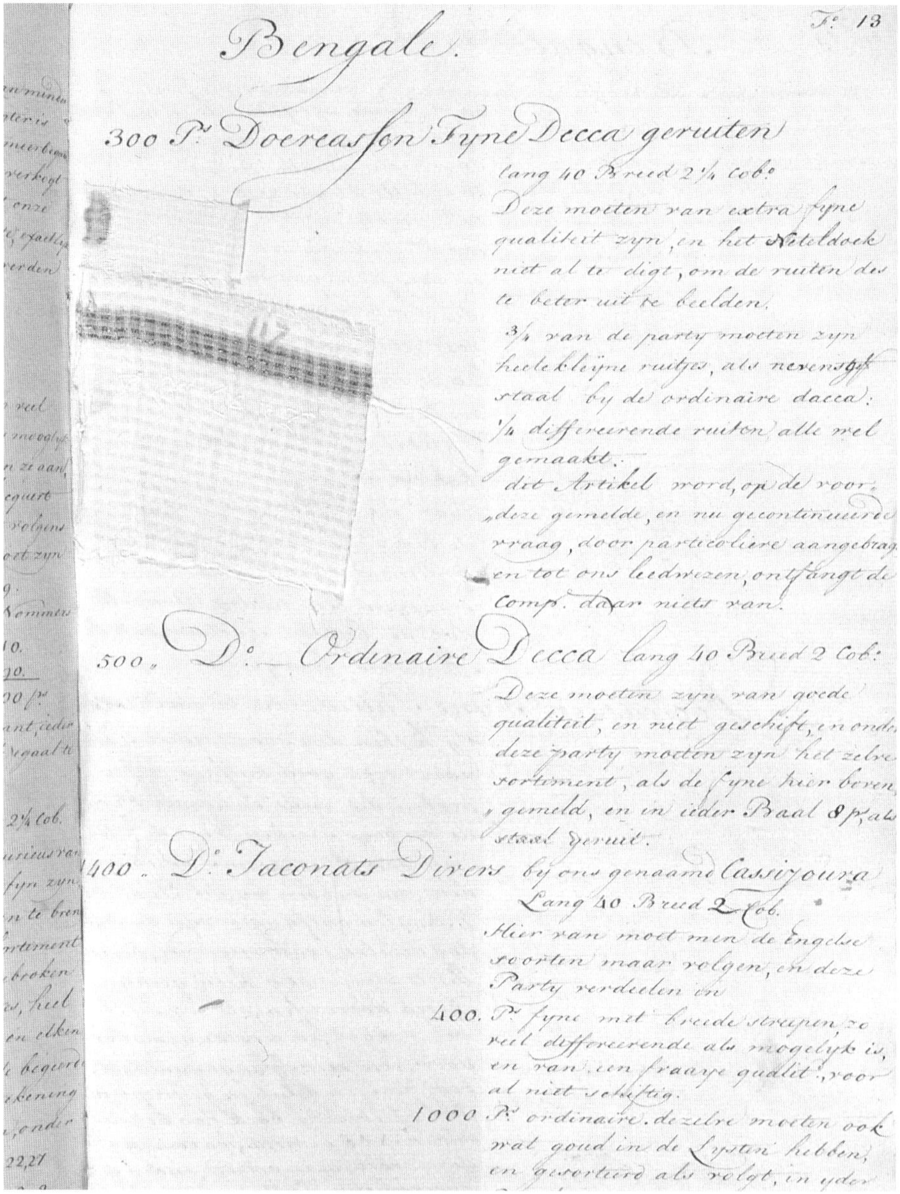
F°. 13

Bengale.

300 P.s Doereas fon Fyne Decca geruiten
lang 40 Breed 2 1/4 Cob°
Deze moeten van extra fyne
qualiteit zyn, en het Neteldoek
niet al te digt, om de ruiten des
te beter uit te beelden.
3/4 van de party moeten zyn
heele kleyne ruitjes, als nevensstaal
staal by de ordinaire dacca:
1/4 differeerende ruiten alle wel
gemaakt.
dit Artikel word, op de voor:
„deze gemelde, en nu gecontinueerde
vraag, door particuliere aangebrag
en tot ons leedwezen, ontfangt de
Comp. daar niets van.

500 „ D° Ordinaire Decca lang 40 Breed 2 Cob:
Deze moeten zyn van goede
qualiteit, en niet geschift, en onder
deze party moeten zyn het zelve
sortiment, als de fyne hier boven
gemeld, en in ieder Baal 8 p.s als
staal deruit.

400 . D° Jaconats Divers by ons genaamd Cassijoura
Lang 40 Breed 2 Cob.
Hier van moet men de Engelse
soorten maar volgen, en deze
Party verdeelen in
400. P.s fyne met breede streepen zo
veel differeerende als mogelyk is,
en van een fraaye qualit.', voor
al niet schiftig.
1000 P.s ordinaire. dezelve moeten ook
wat goud in de Lysten hebben,
en gesorteerd als volgt, in yder

Because of the excellent organisation of the textile trade, the Company successfully reduced the geographical gap between supply and demand, while at the same time bridging the gap in a cultural sense.

The basis of this organisation was the annual *Eis van Retour*, a list drawn up by the Heren XVII of items for the European market that Company officials were to purchase in Asia. The *Eis* was divided into sections for the various VOC districts in Asia. It gave an accurate description of the type, quality and quantity of the required products. Also included was an indication of the price the VOC was prepared to pay. Often, an *Eis* for a consignment of textiles would be accompanied by a sample of the fabric. This might be intended to indicate what the VOC wanted to buy, or alternatively what the Company did not want to buy.

At first VOC merchants purchased their cotton from traders who offered ready-made products for sale in the coastal towns. But as European tastes became more selective it was often necessary to place specific orders with Indian weavers, dyers and painters. This would be arranged through a local intermediary. Yet the time between the receipt of the order and

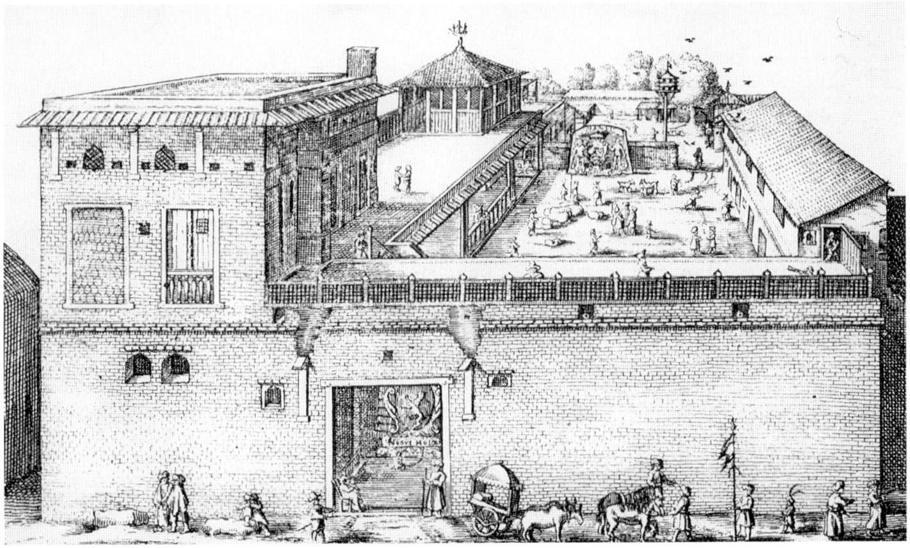

◀ VOC building at the harbour town Surat. The Company opened a trading post here in 1616. Surat developed into a flourishing commercial centre from where large quantities of chintz and brightly coloured materials where shipped to Europe and elsewhere in Asia. When in the early eighteenth century the Mughal Empire began to decline and political unrest in the interior increased, the supply of cotton stagnated. In the course of the eighteenth century Surat was gradually overtaken by Bombay (Mumbai), where the British trading base was located. Engraving from *Begin ende voortgangh...*, 1646.

▼ Negapatnam roadstead. In 1658 the Company captured Negapatnam from the Portuguese and established a factory. In 1690 Negapatnam became the centre of trade on the Coromandel Coast in the southeast of India. Engraving from Wouter Schouten's *Reistogt naar en door Oost-indien...*, 1676.

departure of the ship was often insufficient for the work required. Stocks of plain cotton were therefore maintained which could be decorated as desired immediately after arrival. And to be able to supervise the application of the designs the VOC organised its own workshops.

In some cases, the Company contracted a workshop or even an entire village, including the actual craftsmen to dye and print the cloth under the watchful eye of resident VOC officers. It represented a profound involvement in the Indian textile industry. While in some areas the Com-

pany purchased ready-made fabrics, elsewhere the VOC supervised much of the decoration process and effectively took on the role of producer.

In Amsterdam auctions of the Indian materials purchased and shipped by the VOC were held two or three times a year. These took place at the VOC's linen warehouse neighbouring East India House on Amsterdam's Hoogstraat. Merchants came from throughout Europe to buy chintz and other cotton fabrics. An interesting aspect is the part played by Indian cotton in the West African slave trade, where it was used by the Dutch West India Company to buy slaves. VOC and WIC rubbed shoulders in Amsterdam – their mutual home base and the hub of global commercial activity.

As purchaser and importer of Indian fabrics the VOC exercised a major influence on developments in domestic interiors and clothing in Europe. Chintz was especially popular as upholstery, on bedspreads, bedstead curtains, wall hangings and cushions. It formed an exotic addition to traditional local costumes, like those worn in Hindeloopen, for example. The material was also ideal for jackets, dresses and gowns.

In this way the Company made its mark on European fashions, just as it made its mark on the export production of the Indian textile industry. And literally so on the sample of chintz from Coromandel which was auctioned in February 1783 at the house of the merchant Abraham Ruurds of Leeuwarden: at the bottom left, the sample has the VOC monogram. . . . . .

One particular archaeological find from the wreck of the *Amsterdam* – tobacco – raises some intriguing questions. Where did it come from and where was it originally cultivated? Traces of pollen in this organic material provide some indications. Botanical analysis shows that these remains contain ambrosia and carya pollen. These pollens are typical of the moderate climate of North America: Virginia or Kentucky have therefore been suggested as the probable origin of the tobacco on board the *Amsterdam*.

But elements contained in the find also offer a clue to the route that the tobacco took before eventually finding its way onto the *Amsterdam*. These include the remains of a beetle of the catholethrus species. It is a native of Central and South America, including the Antilles, but is definitely not found north of Mexico. This fact suggests that the tobacco was shipped south from where it is presumed originally to have been grown in North America. A possible scenario is that the tobacco was stored in one of the West India Company's Caribbean entrepôts, perhaps Curaçao or St Eustatius.

It is well-known that Jewish merchants based at the transfer ports on Curaçao and St Eustatius were particularly active in the American tobacco market. With their family connections among the merchants of Amsterdam a network developed that enabled an extensive tobacco trade to emerge. In 1718 there were at least 193 tobacco shops in Amsterdam. One of the principal branches of industry in the city was the processing of the leaves of the plant into snuff and tobacco for smoking. This took place in tobacco spinneries. In 1730 there were thirty of these workshops

◀ Reconstruction of a roll of tobacco as found in the wreck of the *Amsterdam* (sank in 1749). Twisted into strands, the tobacco leaves are held together with sharpened bamboo and ebony pins. Drawing by Eric van Rootselaar, 1995.

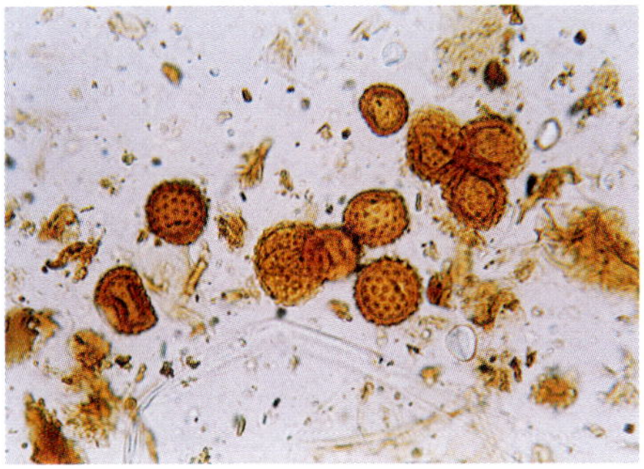

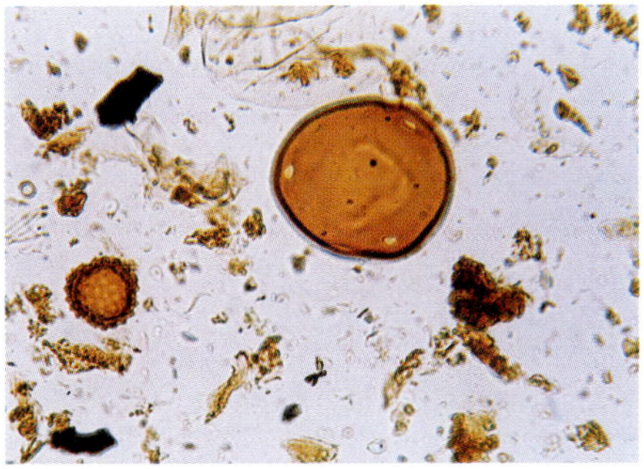

◀ Pollen analysis has revealed that the tobacco from the *Amsterdam* was grown in North America. Examination of the sample revealed pollens of Ambrosia (left) and Carya (hickory), both typical of the vegetation found in the moderate climate of North America. Photo: C.D. Troostheide, IPP University of Amsterdam.

A tobacco workshop around 1700. The women on the right are removing – stripping – the veins from the leaves. The leaves are then twisted on a long work bench. Large, sturdy leaves are laid down, overlapping like roof tiles, with smaller, stripped leaves in between. By revolving a wheel, the leaves are turned into strands. Finally, the strands are wound around an axis to form a roll of tobacco, known as *roltabak*. Engraving from Franz Philipp Florin, *Oeconomus prudens et legalis* (1702).

in Amsterdam. A significant number were run by Jewish entrepreneurs. Here the veins were removed – stripped – from the tobacco leaves. These were then spun on a long work bench. The large, sturdy leaves were laid across each other like roof tiles, and between them smaller stripped tobacco leaves. With the turn of a wheel the leaves were twisted into loose strands. And by twisting the strands around an axis a roll of tobacco was produced. The tobacco found in the wreck of the *Amsterdam* was made in this way and was known as *roltabak*. Interwoven in tresses, the tobacco leaves were kept in place with sharp bamboo and ebony pins.

This explains what happened to the tobacco before the roll was loaded onto the *Amsterdam*. But now a new set of questions arise. Was the *roltabak* for trading or was it part of the *Amsterdam*'s stores, to be rationed out among the crew? Or, alternatively, was it the personal property of one of the higher Dutch East India Company officials sailing on the *Amsterdam*? In fact officers were allowed to take a maximum of 30 pounds of tobacco for their own use on the voyage to Asia. It is also possible that the tobacco was being shipped to Asia as a gift to a local potentate. Or it might have been a means with which to pay the Khoi-Khoi, who supplied services, goods and land to the VOC at the Cape.

No decisive information is available regarding the purpose of the tobacco in the VOC administrative records. It is unclear who delivered the tobacco to the Company. The only entries for tobacco in the accounts are under Roelof Boumeester, supervisor of the slaughterhouse – a section of the VOC concern in Amsterdam; he probably bought tobacco for his own employees to smoke. Another likely candidate is Jurriaan Geijser, who supplied pipes to the Company. He is known to have run a tobacco and tea shop. Whatever the case, the VOC accounts contain just the one payment for the supply of tobacco for an outward-bound ship. This indicates that the VOC kept a store of tobacco for distribution on board. In fact, it was probably part of the rations allocated to the crew of a Company ship.

The VOC Articles, a detailed resume of the rules that applied to the crew on board ship, state that, because of the danger of fire, tobacco could only be smoked on board during the day, 'with the consent and knowledge of the captain, skipper, or commander, and that only in the boarding nets and fore the main mast, ...'. Anyone failing to keep to this strict rule would forfeit a month's salary.

In Amsterdam Adÿ 30 September 1743.

Journal of the senior bookkeeper of the Amsterdam chamber of the VOC, 30 September 1743:

*Paid to Dirck Entvogel, fro 100 gross long fine tobacco pipes at 22 sts. per gross, at f1 pcto nro 372 121.6.-*

Pipe seller Dirck Entvogel sold 100 gross of long fine tobacco pipes at 22 stuivers per gross to the VOC. In the 1740s Entvogel was the principal supplier of pipes to the VOC. Algemeen Rijksarchief, The Hague.

Tobacco was smoked in clay pipes. Between 1740 and 1750 the VOC bought between 100 and 150 gross of pipes a year. These were stocked in barrels, baskets or chests. A packing of buckwheat husks prevented the fragile pipes from breaking during transport. In the eighteenth century Gouda was the principal centre for the manufacture of pipes in Holland. Each pipe maker had a mark which was stamped onto the side or underneath (the heel) of the pipe. In the consignment of pipes found in the wreck of the *Hollandia* (sank in 1743) around 25 different marks have been identified. This is an indication of the number of manufacturers making pipes. In the 1740s the main supplier of pipes to the Company was Dirck Entvogel; he bought his products from a variety of pipe makers.

Other objects associated with tobacco use include tobacco and snuff boxes. The different examples found in the wreck of the *Hollandia* were probably all personal property. To light a pipe a tinderbox was used. These contained tinder which was ignited with a spark from a flint and steel.

All these archaeological finds show that smoking tobacco was part of the daily routine of life on board an eighteenth-century ship. And to an extent it was the VOC that supplied the crew with a ration of tobacco and probably also the pipes with which to smoke it.

A Khoi-Khoi headman with a cow's horn pipe. The VOC often used tobacco to pay the Khoi-Khoi. Known as Hottentots in the days of the Company, they lived in the hinterland surrounding the Cape territory, the area settled by the Company from 1652. Drawing by R.J. Gordon, late eighteenth century.

Ⓐ Caricature of a sailor and a tobacco dealer. The first is smoking a simple clay pipe, the second a wooden pipe with a long stem. Tobacco was a popular stimulant for both rich and poor in the eighteenth century. Anonymous drawing, c. 1700.

# Commerce and arms

## THE MILITARY APPARATUS OF THE VOC



It is an impressive object, the mitre-like hat of red cloth and blue felt. At the front is a copper plate on which a crowned lion clutches a bundle of arrows and a sword in its claws. Below, between two crossed flags, is the VOC emblem with an array of military attributes. Along the edge of the plate are lighted grenades. This represents the Company's military wing – emblazoned on copper.

In the eighteenth century, headgear like this was part of the uniform of the grenadiers employed by the Dutch East India Company. That the Company would have to recruit soldiers was clear from the very start. It was enshrined in the charter of 1602; in the name of the States General the VOC was authorised to enlist 'men of war' and to build fortresses and bastions within the charter territories (that is, between the Cape of Good Hope and the Strait of Magellan). The purpose was also outlined in the charter, namely 'principally for the encouragement of trade'. Commerce – that was the Company's primary concern. But to succeed in trade the VOC needed to have a large military apparatus.

This military aspect is clearly reflected in the composition of the crews that the VOC sent out in its ships. The ship's company was divided into four categories. In the first place, naturally, the sailors who were needed to man the ship. Then there were the craftsmen who performed the specialised technical work. Often East Indiamen would also carry groups of passengers, higher Company officials who were permitted to take their wives and children as well. Finally, a merchantman would have a consignment of soldiers on board. This last category comprised an average of thirty per cent of the total number of people on board. In general, the soldiers on VOC ships would assist in unspecialised jobs, for example by keeping watch. Only in emergencies would they be expected to take on other tasks, for example in a storm when all hands we called on deck or if the crew had been reduced for some reason. Besides defending the ship and the cargo against attack, soldiers were also employed to keep order among the crew. But the soldiers on VOC ships were principally troops *en route* to a posting. Once they were in Asia they would be billeted in one of the many garrisons that the Company maintained throughout its trading empire. By far the largest proportion of the personnel in overseas bases were soldiers.

As was usual in the military world of the seventeenth and eighteenth centuries, the VOC drew many of its recruits from

◀ Grenadier's mitre of a VOC soldier, eighteenth century.

Reconstruction of uniform and equipage of a voc grenadier, eighteenth century. Grenadiers carried a bag with hand grenades. A bag of cartridges was held around the waist with a belt. This contained several prepared cartridges made of a paper tube containing enough gunpowder for a single shot and a round bullet. Grenadiers were armed with a flintlock musket and a dagger. Drawing Paul Maas, 1995.

men who originated outside the Republic. Indeed, the same applied to the Company's sailors; in the eighteenth century half the crews were of foreign extraction. The share of foreigners among the military personnel in the same century actually rose to three-quarters. These were people from the lowest social classes, a collection of riffraff whom the ships surgeon Nicolaes de Graaff described in his *Oost-Indische Spiegel* as 'all kinds of strange and alien nations such as Poles, Swedes, Danes, Norwegians, Jutes, Hamburgers, Bremers, Lubeckers, Danzigers, Koningsbergers, High Germans, Easterners, Westphalians, Bergers, Juliers, Clevens, and all manner of Huns, Papists, Krauts, country yokels and other green Kassupers with the grass still stuck between their teeth'. The voc had its own veritable foreign legion which for major military operations in Asia was augmented with oriental auxiliaries.

At first the Company's Asian activities involved sailing from port to port: the voc was a mobile force. Later, once the Com-

Ⓐ Cavalry officer and horseman from Malabar (in Southwest India). Besides European soldiers the Company also drew many of its military recruits from Asia. Drawing by Jan Brandes, second half eighteenth century.

pany had established a foothold on *terra firma*, trading posts began to appear throughout Asia. In the second half of the seventeenth century a period of aggressive expansion followed, accompanied by major military operations. In some areas this led to political claims on territory by the VOC – particularly on Ceylon (Sri Lanka) and Java. Gradually, the VOC acquired the role of autocratic ruler, a matter in the seventeenth century for which the Honourable Company received unreserved praise, as the following illustrates: 'From small beginnings, today the Company has by God's grace climbed and reached so high that all the principal sums invested have multiplied many times. The same Company raises troops at own cost, fields armies, defeats them, disbands, wages war in other worlds, conquers cities, overwhelms islands, launches fleets, imposes its will on enemy nations, castles, roadsteads and harbours [...] does and causes things that are little different from the powers of great Kings and Rulers.' But in the eighteenth century the maintenance of the political-military constellation that others had built up before began to weigh heavily on the Company. The debilitating wars against the local potentates of Ceylon and Java led to gigantic increases in costs.

The characteristic twin roles of the VOC – as both merchant and soldier – had been enshrined in the charter of 1602. This double role appeared to have a tenacity all its own. An eighteenth-century observer noted that the VOC acted in Asia like a

Three European VOC soldiers. The military character of the Company is evident from the fact that the majority of European personnel stationed in the overseas bases were soldiers. These included many Germans and Scandinavians. Anonymous drawing, eighteenth century Algemeen Rijksarchief, The Hague.

sovereign, although one whose head was on a merchant's body. If war, according to Clausewistz' famous formulation, is the continuation of politics by other means, for the VOC it was the continuation of trade by other means. Indeed, that was how the charter described it: war 'for the encouragement of trade'.

# Profits and piety



A rectangular, openwork plate with two figures surrounded by decoration bearing the Dutch East India Company monogram – this is a lectern from the Amsterdam chamber, probably intended for a Bible or a psalter from which the lesson was read in a Protestant church service. Here the VOC monogram supports the message of the Gospel: clearly religion was a matter that the Company took seriously.

Critical or ill-disposed foreigners often claimed that for the Dutch profit was more important than piety. But while the charter of 1602 may not have specified provisions regarding religion, from the start this was an area which received the fullest attention from the directors – as the official correspondence shows. During the two hundred years of its existence the VOC sent out hundreds of Calvinist ministers and thousands of lay preachers and schoolmasters. This was all at the Company's own expense. And that included the costs of supporting these people while they remained in Asia. At the same time, the Heren XVII also provided funds for churches and schools. In Batavia and Colombo seminaries were founded to train candidates as preachers. Moreover, the VOC financed the printing and distribution of Bibles and other morally uplifting literature, in Dutch and in Asian languages.

Just as the VOC established certain ground rules that enabled religious life on board ship and in the overseas bases to continue, they also laid down definite limits to religious involvement. In a way, the Company's religious policies were an extension of the State's preeminence over the Church. There was never any question of equal status for religion and commerce within the Company. Whenever the (commercial) interests of the Company clashed with religious interests, it was always the Church that drew the short straw. 'The nature of government is such that it cannot tolerate two equally dominant sovereign powers, just as a single body cannot have two heads', the directors in the Republic wrote to Governor General Joan Maetsuyker and his council on 12 April 1656. In the VOC it was the merchant, not the preacher who determined policy.

Instead of leaving appointments and transfers to the Church, the Heren XVII insisted that their own governors in Asia decide on the tenures of ministers and lay preachers. All church councils were supposed to include a secular VOC official; and the approval of these lay members was required for a resolution to be passed. The government in Batavia also had the right

❮ Lectern with VOC monogram, Amsterdam, eighteenth century.

▲ Local potentate from Golconda in India attending the Dutch Reformed church in Masulipatnam on the Coromandel Coast in Southeast India. Engraving from D. Havart, *Op- en ondergang van Coromandel*, 1693. Netherlands Maritime Museum, Amsterdam.

to examine and censor correspondence by ministers and church committees from the East to the Republic. In effect, the directors treated ministers and lay preachers as paid subordinates. And like every other VOC employee, their position was enshrined in the rigid hierarchy that characterised the Company's personnel structure.

Ministers and lay preachers were charged in the first placed with the pastoral care and ministry to the personnel of the Company on the long voyages and during their stay in the tropics, maintaining general standards of decency, discipline and morality was also central to their assignment. That was no easy task, however; after all,

In 1661 a number of preachers and almoners in the service of the VOC were tortured and eventually killed on Formosa (Taiwan) by local warriors. Conversion and the spread of Dutch education on Formosa was comparatively successful until 1662 when the VOC finally lost power on the island. Anonymous engraving, second half seventeenth century.

the soldiers and sailors who worked for the Company had not earned their reputation without reason: an assortment of lowlifes, generally thought of as the dregs of Dutch society. The difficult circumstances of the job made a position as a preacher with the VOC far from attractive. In fact it was a constant battle to attract sufficient numbers to fill the various religious posts. Moreover, the prospect of being completely subservient to the civil apparatus of the VOC could hardly have made the ostensibly attractive idea of an Asian parish particularly inviting.

To ensure that the religious needs of the Company officials were served, the VOC was often forced to take on individuals whose spiritual calling left much to be desired. The lower ranks of church assistants – lay readers and visitors or comforters of the sick – received a particularly poor press. They were recruited from the working classes and could boast only a bare minimum of theological knowledge. On board ship their role was that of a kind of chaplain. On land they would be appointed as a schoolmaster or hospital visitor. The complaints about them were legion; in 1614 Jan Pietersz Coen described them as 'rude, crude idiots'.

Besides providing pastoral care for Company personnel, these ministers of religion had another task, a calling of a higher order: that of bringing the Gospel to the indigenous population of Asia. But a variety of factors combined to prevent the successful spread of Protestantism in the East. Most obviously, in many places Catholicism had already established a firm foothold. This had been the work of the Portuguese who had taken their missionary task far more seriously in an earlier period. Moreover, compared to the Baroque splendour of Catholic religious ceremony the sobriety of the Calvinist rite must have seemed rather less enticing. For many Asians Protestantism was not an attractive alternative. At the same time, the Dutch preachers who arrived in areas where the VOC operated encountered deeply rooted religions such as Islam, Hinduism and Buddhism. Nevertheless, these evangelists achieved successes in several parts of Asia: on Formosa (Taiwan), Ceylon (Sri Lanka) and Ambon large numbers of native islanders were converted to Christianity.

Yet, apart from Ambon – where a lively Protestant tradition has survived to this day – Calvinism made little permanent headway among the Asian peoples of the tropics where the VOC preached the Gospel. And this while from the very start of Dutch overseas expansion part of the intention had been to bring 'the light of the true faith' to Asia's population. 'Moral education of the islander', the basic premise of Dutch ethical policy in the colonies around 1900, went back a long way. But that the Company's merchants never lost sight of the need for commercial profit is evident, for example, from the enthusiasm with which the VOC organised ships to ferry Islamic pilgrims to the holy city of Mecca. No one could construe this lucrative sideline as sign of Christian piety. . . . . .

# God's word in Arabic

As the age of the trading companies took hold, the commercial contacts between Europe and Asia were accompanied by the first, cautious cultural exchanges between the two continents. Part of this cultural traffic resulted in the production of an Arabic printed letter type about the size of a matchstick head.

One of these letters was found in the wreck of the *Hollandia* (sank in 1743). Shortly before, the Dutch East India Company had purchased a set of Augustijn Maleijts type from the Amsterdam firm of Voskes en Clerk. Additional equipment for printing books found in the wreck came from Arent Smits, another Amsterdam establishment. This eighteenth-century printing-press maker sold two 'book printing presses' to the Amsterdam chamber in June 1743 for ƒ220 each. The type and presses were for a planned new printing works in Batavia. The initiative for this so-called seminary printshop came from the newly appointed Governor General Gustaaf Willem van Imhoff (1743-1750). Apart from providing new Dutch texts, the press was also intended to produce texts in Malay. Shortly after the loss of the *Hollandia*, the VOC ordered new presses and sets of type; these eventually arrived at their destination and in 1744 the seminary press – which had opened that same year – printed a proof sheet with the Augustijn Maleijts letters. Two years later a Catechism appeared, commissioned by Van Imhoff and printed by Harmanus Mulder, the head of the seminary printshop.

This Catechism represents a milestone in the cultural exchange between Europe and Asia: it was the first Christian text printed in Arabic letters commissioned by the VOC. European (Christian) texts had been printed in Malay before 1744, but this had always been in roman type – a transliteration into Western script. These texts included all kinds of auxiliary signs to help Europeans reading them to pronounce the words with the correct Malay intonation. By producing a Catechism in Arabic script the VOC ensured that the local population – at least those who were literate – would be able to read the Christian texts themselves. Van Imhoff's evangelist zeal was unique in that this was the first time such a far-reaching adaptation had been made to the needs of the indigenous population. Before, they had always had to adapt to European standards.

From the start, the VOC saw the spread of the Dutch Reformed faith as an important task. It was one of the instructions given by the Heren XVII to the first governor of the East Indies. As early as 1603 the

◀ Type with Arabic character found in the wreck of the *Hollandia* (sank in 1743).

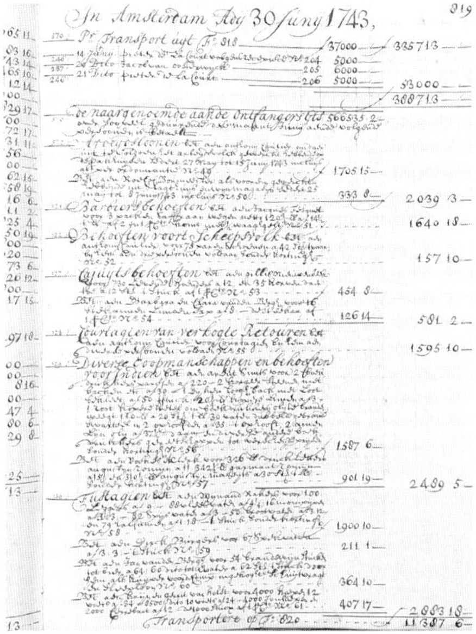


Company sought 'two capable men to bring God's word to the peoples of the Indies and to warn them against the superstitions and temptations of Moors and atheists with the Holy Scriptures'.

To reach these peoples of the Indies it was necessary to speak the local languages. In the East Indian archipelago, long the centre of the Company's empire, this was Malay, the language spoken in parts of Sumatra and the Malaysian peninsula and which was understood by traders in practically every coastal town. In 1611 the first Malay booklet appeared in Amsterdam

**A** Journal of the senior bookkeeper of the Amsterdam Chamber of the voc, 30 June 1743.

*Diverse merchandise and requirements for the Indies paid to Arent Smits, for 2 book-printing presses at f220, 2 proof plates with trays etc: at f30.-: 1 oak lye bath lined with lead at f50; 20 lb copper lines at f3; 1 red copper kettle to boil the book-printer's oil, weighing 110 £ at 20 st. per £, 30 vats twice-burned lampblack ink in 2 barrels at f35: the barrel, two 2 vats of linseed oil at f37; the vat and diverse other book-printers tools at various prices without reductions no. 56 f1,587 6/- Paid to Voskes & Clerk, for 326 £ print letters augustijn Romijn, at 11; 342 £ garmant Romijn at f15 and 310 £ augustijn Maleijts at 30 st. per £. Without reductions no. 57 901 19/-*

Amsterdam printing press manufacturer Arent Smits supplied two presses to the voc with 'two proof plates and trays' (flat stones on which the setter could correct a set text). In addition a lye bath: a basin lined with lead to clean the form with the letters when set, and copper lines with texts containing lines – like tables – was set. He also sold ingredients for making printing ink – linseed oil and lampblack – and a copper pot in which the heat these. The voc bought letters for setting the text from Voskes en Clerk: the Augustijn Romijn (12 point), the smaller Garmant Romijn and the Augustijn Maleijts, an Arabic type. Algemeen Rijksarchief, The Hague.

(it had just fourteen pages) financed by Albert Cornelis Ruyl, who had visited Ambon in the employ of the VOC. It contained the Ten Commandments, the Catechism and a series of psalms. Some twenty years later in Enkhuizen the printer Jacob Palenstein produced a New Testament in Dutch and Malay, 'translated from the Greek original'. In fact the title promised more than the book delivered; it only contained Matthew.

Later a serious attempt was made to translate the Bible into Malay, this time both the Old and New Testament – complete. The church council in Batavia, which came under direct authority of the VOC, commissioned Dr Melchior Leijdecker in 1691. Leijdecker took the task to heart and applied himself with diligence. After many delays, in 1733 – by which time Leijdecker had died – the job was finished. The whole Malay Bible was printed in Amsterdam by R. and G. Wetstein. As the Heren XVII had already resolved, the edition was printed in Western roman type. Leijdecker's Bible translation remained in use for many years; it continued to be reprinted until into the twentieth century. On the Moluccan islands, where the largest number of converts was made, Leijdecker's Bible acquired a status similar to the Staten Bible in the Netherlands.

PROEF VAN LETTEREN

Die te bekomen zyn, by

VOSKES EN CLERK.

GR. CAN. ROMYN.
Pax una triumphis innumeris potior. Nulla salus bello. n

Gr. Canon Curfyf.
*Melior est umbra senum in civitate, quam gladius juvenum.*

KL. CANON ROMYN.
Præter Reformatos alios etiam Sarvivius Parlamenti antehac Rotomagensis, nunc Paisiensis consi

Klyne Canon Curfyf.
*Da pacem Domine, in Diebus nostris: quia non est alius, qui pugnet pro nobis, nisi tu Deus noster.*

ASCENDONICA ROMYN.
Periclitatur Castitas in deliciis, Humilitas in divitiis, Varitas in multiloquio, Pietas in negotio. Rem tuam custodi.
ÆABCDEFGHIKLM.

Ascendonica Curfyf.
*Filius est Spes parentum, Memoria nominis, Subsidium generis, Heres familiæ, Reipublicæ civis Sapiens animum intuetur, donm*
*ÆABCDEFGHIJKL.*

GR. PARAGON ROMYN.
Nihil pejus est iis, qui paulum aliqui ultra primas literas progressi, falsam sibi scientiæ persuasionem induerunt. Numm
ABCDEFGHIKLMN

KL. PARAGON ROMYN.
Tota philosophorum vita est Commentatio mortis. Infertum est, quam longa nostrum cujusque vita futura sit. Virtutem incolumen odi-
ABCDEFGHIJKLMNOP

Paragon Curfyf.
*Omnes homines summa ope niti decet, ne vitam silentio transigant veluti pecora. Vita humana vitiis interit, Virtute conservatur. Scopus vitæ Christus*
*ABCDEFGIHKLMNOPR*

GROOTE TEXT ROMYN.
Væ miseris ovibus, ubi Judex est Lupus. Væ bono, cum legem fert malus. Veritas parit odium. Misericordia non causam, sed miseriam spectat. Facilius est, suadere patientiam, quam pati. Artes &
ABCDEFGHIKLMNOPRSZ

KLYNE TEXT ROMYN.
Frequens usus omnium magistrorum præcepta superat. Pecuniam in loco negligere maximum quandoque est lucrum. Omnia si perdas, famam servare memento, qua semel amissa, postea nullus eris.
ABCDEFGHIKLMNOPQRSTV

Text Curfyf.
*Quicunque non docet filium suum aliquam artem vel officium, per inde est, ac si doceat eum latrocinari. Natura tenaſſimi sumus eorum quæ, rudibus annis percepimus. Multum loquentiæ, parum sapientiæ.*
*ÆABCDEFGHIJKLMNOQ*

Nog zyn t'Amsterdam op de Agterburgwal, over't Prinçe-Hof; by dezelve te bekomen: Hebreeusche, Griexe, Hoog-en Nederduytse, van groot tot klein; en verscheyden Orientaalse Letteren, &c.

**A** Specimen of types from the early eighteenth century, cast by the Amsterdam type casters Voskes en Clerk, including augustijn Romijn. This was the type supplied to the VOC, as noted in the bookkeeper's journal of June 1743. Of the various 'Oriental letters' mentioned in the bottom line, the VOC bought the Arabic type. Joh. Enschedé en Zonen collection, Haarlem.

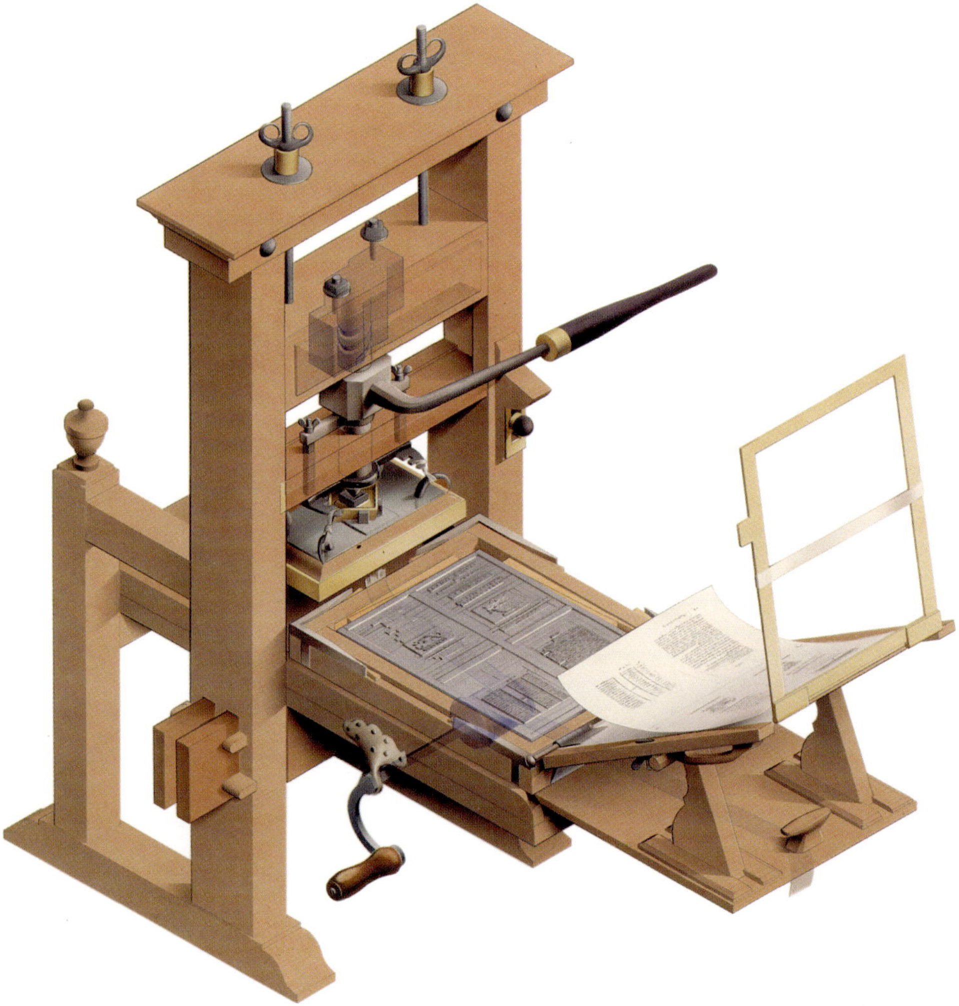

Once again, it was the overseas section of the VOC, in the person of Governor General Jacob Mossel, who first encouraged the printing of Leijdecker's Bible translation in Arabic Malay script. That was in 1758, twelve years after Van Imhoff's Catechism had appeared. The spread of Western cultural influence in the East, or at least attempts to achieve this, made slow but steady progress.

The VOC played an active role in the publication of books in foreign languages and scripts, not just Malay, but also Portuguese, Tamil, Singhalese and even the Singkiang dialect spoken on Formosa. The international nature of trade ensured that the Company developed as a multilingual enterprise. In that sense, as the focus of interchange between East and West, it was the VOC that first initiated the process of globalization. The letter from the *Hollandia* was a tiny, but significant link in that process.

Reconstruction of an eighteenth-century printing press. Drawing by Paul Maas, 1995.

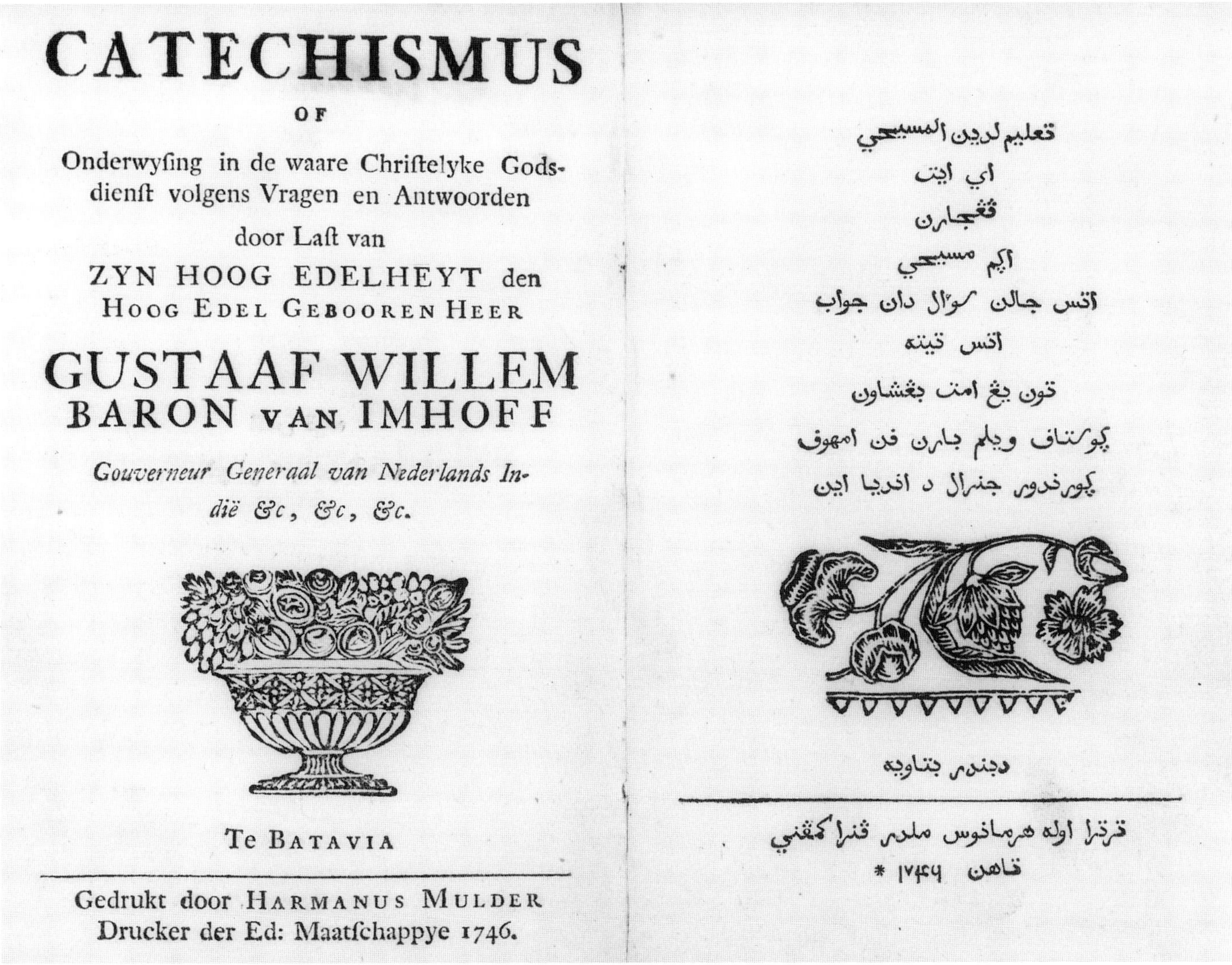

CATECHISMUS

OF

Onderwyſing in de waare Chriſtelyke Gods-dienſt volgens Vragen en Antwoorden

door Laſt van

ZYN HOOG EDELHEYT den

HOOG EDEL GEBOOREN HEER

GUSTAAF WILLEM

BARON VAN IMHOFF

*Gouverneur Generaal van Nederlands Indië &c, &c, &c.*

Te BATAVIA

Gedrukt door HARMANUS MULDER

Drucker der Ed: Maatſchappye 1746.

تعليم لدين المسيحي

اي ايت

ڤغجارن

اڬم مسيحي

اتس جالن سؤال دان جواب

اتس تيته

توان يغ امت بغشاون

ڬوستاف ويلم بارن فن امهوف

ڬوبرندور جنرال د اندريا اين

دبندر بتاويه

ترترا اوله هرمانوس ملدر ڤنرا كمڤني

تاهن ١٧٤٦ *

A Titlepage of the Catechism, printed in 1746 by the seminary printshop in Batavia, commissioned by Governor General G.W. van Imhoff. The Malay text is printed in Arabic type.

# Other end of the world



If there was one place that could be identified as the nerve centre of the Dutch East India Company, it was East India House in Amsterdam. It was here that the directors of the Amsterdam chamber of the VOC met twice each week. It was also here that the Heren XVII, (the directors of the VOC) gathered for their meetings. These happened twice a year and they generally continued for a matter of weeks. The rules stated that these be rotated in turn: six successive years in Amsterdam, then two years in Middelburg.

East India House was therefore the main location where the trade of this worldwide enterprise was managed. It was the focus of power, its influence extending across enormous distances to the farthest corners of the globe. In 1663 Olfert Dapper described the great hall of East India House where the 'assembly of seventeen' determined their policy: 'Hanging in the hall where the Directors meet and debate their business, there are splendid Chinese and Japanese paintings. Also hanging in the hall is the great city of Batavia, with its terrifying and invincible castle. And there is the royal court of Japan, without equal anywhere in the world in worth, size and strength. Hanging all around are the islands of the Moluccas, fortresses, orchards filled with spice trees, cities, harbours, capes that we occupy at the other end of the world.'

The actual operation of Company business was left to the more adventurous employees in Asia; few of the directors had ever seen the exotic locations where the VOC bases were established with their own eyes. The paintings on the wall of the great hall described by Dapper gave them some idea about the places 'at the other end of the world' about which they made decisions in their meetings. For the directors back in the Dutch Republic these paintings formed a two-dimensional window on their international trading empire.

The term empire is perhaps a little misleading in this case. Dutch expansion in the seventeenth and eighteenth centuries, with the financially powerful VOC in the vanguard, may have been worldwide, but it was also superficial. If this was an empire it was one of dots and dashes. The dashes represented the trading routes controlled by the VOC; the dots the Company's overseas bases. During the two centuries of its existence the VOC held some 300 of these bases or factories – some operating for a short period, others for longer. The differences between these locations were enormous: one might be a single office where as few as four VOC merchants wor-

◀ View of Batavia Castle. In the seventeenth and eighteenth centuries, the painting hung in the great hall of East India House in Amsterdam.
Paitning by Andries Beeckman, 1657 (?).

Meeting with Stadholder William v as principal director of the Amsterdam chamber of the voc, 1 June 1768. On the walls in this drawing of the great hall of East India House in Amsterdam are paintings, including Beeckman's view of the castle of Batavia.
Copy after a drawing by Simon Fokke, 1771.

ked; another might be a solid bulwark of European power where a large body of civil Company employees was backed by a major garrison of troops.

Batavia was of course an example of the latter category. At a central point in the great hall of East India House, above the fireplace, hung a painting showing the Castle of Batavia that the voc had built. Within the wall of this bastion sat the governor general and his council, together forming the government of the East, and as such exercising direct authority over the Company's overseas enterprises. Batavia also functioned as the *rendez-vous* for the voc fleet. The products bought in the various Asian regions were shipped to Batavia from where these were transhipped to Europe or elsewhere in Asia.

Despite the European appearance of many of the buildings, and the institutions based on the Dutch civic apparatus – the town council and the public orphanage – there were only a relatively small number of Europeans living in this ostensibly Dutch settlement. Around 1700 there were some 70,000 people living in and around Batavia; 6,000 of these were of European origin. In the course of the eighteenth century the number of Europeans declined, while the total number of inhabitants of the town increased. The population was remarkable for its diversity. Groups of people from various parts of the archipelago lived side-by-side in *kampongs* on the outskirts of the city. After 1680 the Chinese began to settle in Batavia in significant numbers; they formed the largest population group and contributed in a unique way to the city's development. In fact, three hundred years ago Batavia was more a Chinese than a Dutch colonial city.

Nevertheless, as the administrative, managerial and maritime centre of the VOC's Asian operation, Batavia far exceeded the other overseas posts and settlements of the Company in size and importance. Many of the factories comprised no more than a few buildings where a small number of Europeans resided in completely alien surroundings. In Asia, where the frequency of sea-going traffic was determined by the changing monsoon winds, most trade was seasonal. This meant that Company employees in most factories would be especially busy during the trading season. But once the ships had been loaded and had sailed off, there was little to do until the next season began. In the off-season period, life in some of the more isolated factories and outposts must have represented an unpleasant and dull existence, with almost no contact with the outside world. Isaac Titsingh, director of Bengal, wrote in 1786 from his base Chinsura: 'Since my arrival here I have found little enjoyment; the landscape, which many appreciate, I do not like; I have little taste in company, every day one meets the same people, among whom hate and envy ensuing from former troubles are kept alive for ages; it is like a purgatory in which it is my task to open the doors to Paradise so that trade can pick up again ...'. The reality emerges: behind the history of the VOC – which some modern observers see as a large, all-embracing adventure – there is the far less spectacular everyday history of individuals plagued by endless boredom.

THEODORA,
HENDRICA,
PIEKENBROEK,
IN,LEEVEN,HUYSVROUW,
VAN,D,AGTBR: HEER,BOUDEWYN,
VERSELEWEL,FAURE,OUD,EERSTE,
SECERETARIS,VAN,D: HOOGE,REGERING,
EN,DIRECTEUR, VAN,BENGALEN,
GEBOREN,TOT, BATAVIA,
DEN,25 JULY ANNO 1746
OBIIT,TOT,BENGALEN,DEN
27 MAART,Ao 1770 OUD
23 JAAREN 8 MAANDEN
EN,6 DAAGEN

# Women and the company



Focussing on the material remains of the Dutch East India Company, it is easy to forget that for two hundred years it was people who kept the machinery turning as best as they could. People employed by the VOC. In the middle of the eighteenth century, when the Company reached the height of its expansion, there were some 3,000 employees at the offices, shipyards and warehouses in the Republic, while 12,000 sailors manned the VOC fleet. In the overseas bases there were around

Memorial plaque commemorating Theodora Hendrica Piekenbroek which hung in the Dutch church in Chinsura (Bengal).

Memorial plaque commemorating Boudewijn Verselewel Faure which hung in the Dutch church in Chinsura (Bengal).

25,000 Company employees. More than 17,000 of these were of European extraction. Throughout its two hundred years the VOC maintained the communication lines between Europe and Asia with hardly any interruptions. Almost a million Europeans left the Low Countries for a short or extended stay, sailing on one of the total of 4,789 passages that the VOC's ships made to Asia.

Only a tiny percentage of these people were women. Among the spectacular examples are the women stowaways who made their way on board VOC ships. In the Dutch Republic women, disguised as men, would sign up and join a ship as a sailor or soldier. In the course of the voyage to Asia their true identity would eventually become known and cause havoc among the ship's company for the remainder of the journey. The reason for this reckless behaviour would often be the presence of a lover on board. The lower ranks – sailors, soldiers and craftsmen – were not allowed to take their wives to sea. At the same time, the realisation that a woman of low social status would have a reasonable chance of marrying a well-heeled VOC employee once out East led many an enterprising young woman to attempt a clandestine crossing. Women stowaways on VOC ships were recorded almost every year. Yet these women represent only a fraction of the European women who emigrated to Asia in this period.

It was in 1627 that the first wife of a prominent Company employee came from Europe to Batavia. She was Eva Ment, wife of Jan Pieterszoon Coen, who had just begun his second term as governor general. Coen was setting an example. The influx of women and even entire families from the Republic was supposed to ensure that European communities would flourish in the Company's overseas posts. To encourage this, in 1622 Coen had developed a remarkable initiative that involved the transport of marriageable young women from Amsterdam's orphanages. Four VOC ships were allocated for the purpose. How many of these orphans actually made it to Batavia is not recorded. However, thirty young women sailed on the *Leiden*, of whom Coen was later able to report that all had been honourably married to VOC officers. As an organisation, however, the VOC was not designed to transport women, and Coen's grand plans for a tight-knit community of Dutch families in the East never materialised.

Never in the VOC's history could the family be said to have been the cornerstone of colonial society. In the VOC's Asian bases unmarried relationships existed side-by-side with marriages. Because of the absence of European women, many Company employees had relationships with local women. Some became marriages if the woman was a Christian, but often the woman was treated as property, being perhaps of simple origins and hardly distinguishable from the household servants. Yet it was in the domestic environment that many of the European Company employees became acquainted with genuine Asian culture: the food, clothing, sanitation and other aspects of daily life. Daughters of mixed parents tended towards the culture of their mothers or nurses far more than sons. This resulted in the continuation of the native element in colonial society as the pattern was repeated from generation to generation. The private circumstances of the VOC employees who worked overseas ensured that a liaison with the Asian world occurred on a domestic level. It led to an unusual cultural development. Instead of creating a New Netherlands in the tropics, the Dutch colonists gradually abandoned the influences of the motherland.

Despite their decisive influence on the everyday life of Company employees in Asia, women led an anonymous existence in colonial society, excluded from the business of the VOC and the trading and communications of the Company. One woman's identity has been rescued from obscurity: Theodora Hendrica Piekenbroek. Theodora was the daughter of Gerrit Piekenbroek, a preacher in Batavia, and Ulrica Helena Pfeil. She was born and raised in Batavia and died and buried in Bengal. Theodora was European, although she never saw Europe with her own eyes.

In Batavia on 22 April 1762 Theodora Hendrica Piekenbroek married Boudewijn Verselewel Faure, then senior merchant with the VOC. Boudewijn, born on 25 January 1734 in Dendermonde, arrived in the East Indies in 1756 on the *Brouwer*. After a successful career in the VOC administration in Batavia he was eventually appointed director of Bengal on 18 July 1769. A number of crucial VOC trading posts were situated in this area of Northeast India, where large amounts of textiles were purchased. The key base was a place called Chinsura on the river Hooghly, where around 250 Company employees worked. Here Faure settled together with his wife. It was to be his final posting in a long and successful international career with the Company. But on 12 May 1770, less than a year after his appointment, the new director died following a short illness. His wife had succumbed even earlier to the oppressive heat of Chinsura. Theodora

A Jan Pietersz Coen (1587-1629), Governor General (1619-1623 and 1627-1629). Based on an initiative by Coen, in 1622 marriageable young women were shipped over from Amsterdam's orphanages to Java. The Governor General hoped that this would help create a Dutch community in Batavia.
Anonymous painting, mid-seventeenth century.

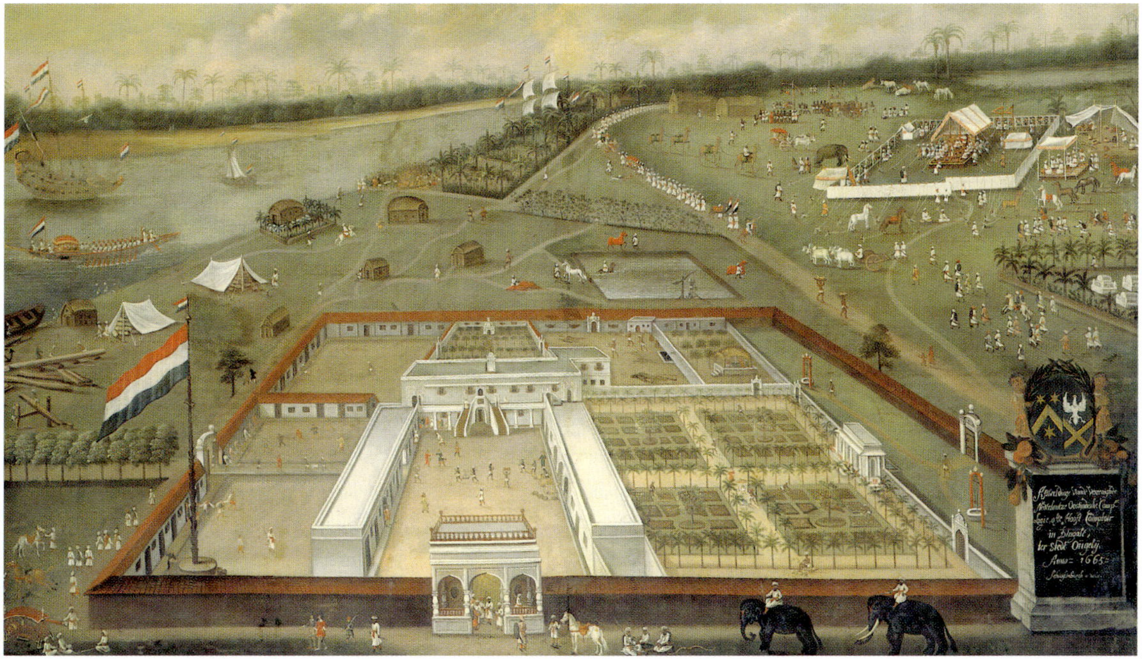

Hendrica Piekenbroek died on 27 March 1770. She was only 23 years old.

After their death memorial plaques were made for both husband and wife. Together with plaques commemorating other Company employees who passed away in Chinsura, they adorned the walls of the Dutch church which stood here in the middle of the eighteenth century. These were modest and personal commemorations that recalled just some of the many who served as employees of the Company and died in a strange world far from home.

**A** View of the voc base in Chinsura on the river Hooghly. In 1770 Boudewijn Verselewel Faure and his wife Theodora Hendrica Piekenbroek died in Chinsura. The couple had lived in the place for less than a year.
Painting by Hendrick van Schuylenburgh, 1665.